MW00712138

COLUMBIA
city of rivers, vistas and dreams

famously Hot!

by Tom Poland
with an introduction by
Dr. Harris Pastides

J Robert Towery — Publisher, Editor, & Art Director
James Tomlinson — Executive Publisher
Ardith Bradshaw — Editor
Nikki Sepsis — Profile Editor

Published by
a division of the Publishing Resources Group, Inc.
Jacques Verhaak, President & CFO
www.pubresgroup.com

URBAN Renaissance Books

A City of Rivers,

Photo by Brian Dressler

Vistas & Dreams

Photo by Jay Browne

THE CONGAREE RIVER, COLUMBIA BORN, FORMS UP NEAR THE FALL LINE WHERE THE SALUDA AND BROAD RIVERS MERGE AND SHAPES THE CITY'S WESTERN EDGE. ◄

OUR NATIONAL SYMBOL CRUISES THE CONGAREE RIVER, JOINED NOW AND THEN BY OSPREY, AND RARER STILL BY THE SWALLOW-TAILED KITE—ALL FISH THE RIVER'S SHOALS.. ▲

THE DAWNING OF A SALUDA RIVER MORNING. ▼

Photo by Jay Browne

Famously Hot!

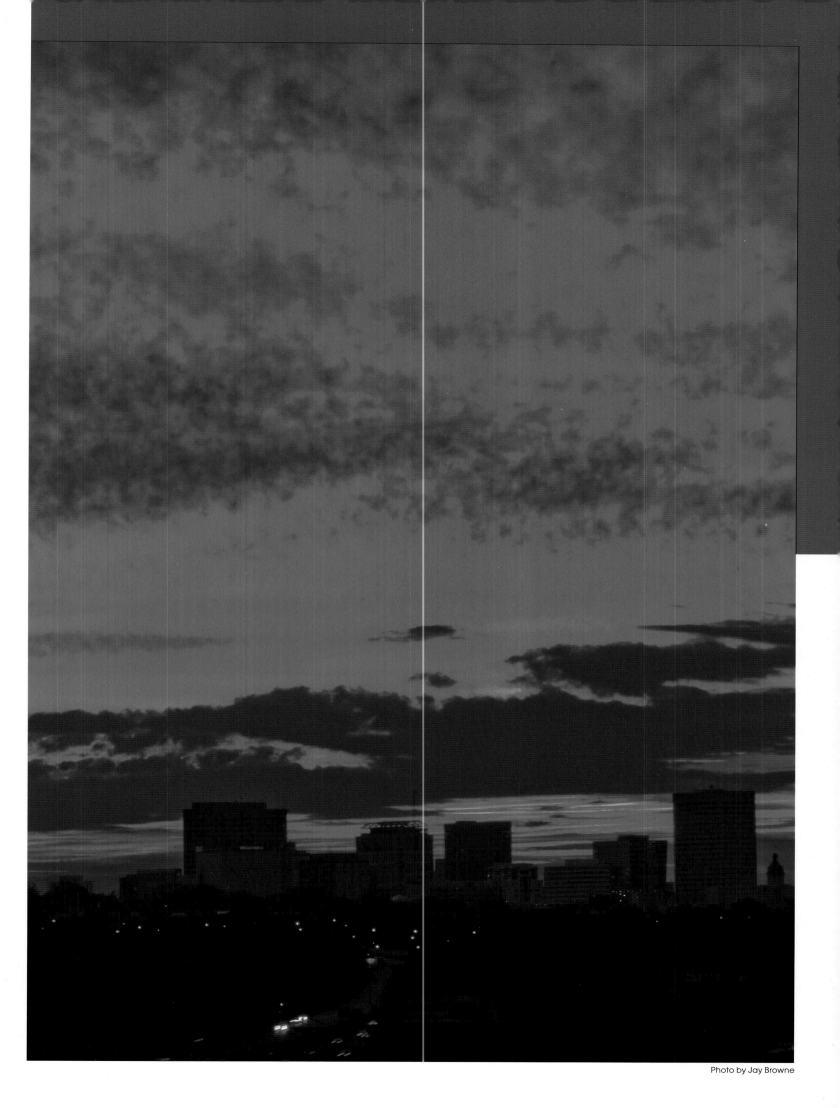

Photo by Jay Browne

Photo by Jay Browne

COLUMBIA
city of rivers, vistas and dreams

Library of Congress Control Number: 2014956787

Poland, Tom 1954 COLUMBIA—CITY OF RIVERS, VISTAS, AND DREAMS celebrates this storied capital, describing its abundance of lush public parks, sparkling cool rivers that spill into the heart of the city, art museums and a zoo and public gardens comparable to those in cities much larger and, allegedly, more urbane. The book also includes a photo-journal of this vibrant community, documenting how it continues to nurture the dreams of all its very fortunate–and famously hot–citizens.

COPYRIGHT © 2015 BY PUBLISHING RESOURCES GROUP, INC. ALL RIGHTS RESERVED. No part of this work may be reproduced or copied in any form or by any means, except for brief excerpts in conjunction with book reviews, without prior written permission of the publisher.

PUBLISHED BY
A DIVISION OF THE PUBLISHING RESOURCES GROUP, INC.
w w w . p u b r e s g r o u p . c o m
URBANRenaissanceBOOKS
ISBN # 978-0-9847145-6-8   Printed in South Korea

Contents

Helen Evans, owner of Amazin' Gracie Photography, created the front cover photo. This dawn view of the Gervais Street Bridge captures the spirit of Columbia and embodies our title—-a vista revealing the Congaree River in dreamy relief.
http://amazingraciephotography.zenfolio.com/

Jay Browne, Jay Browne Photography, captured the back-cover photo. This dawn image summons the feeling that Columbians call home and speaks to the bright future toward which the community is striving.
jayandturbo@gmail.com

A City on the Move

Dr. Harris Pastides

Patricia and I moved from Amherst, Massachusetts to Columbia, South Carolina in the summer of 1998. I had accepted a position as the new Dean of the Arnold School of Public Health and we were excited to join the University of South Carolina family. We had never lived in the South and, to be honest, we weren't quite sure what to expect. I suppose we had anticipated a hospitable but sleepy college town and a quiet, provincial life. What we discovered, however, was quite different—Columbia was a vibrant, hospitable mid-sized city with a big heart and big plans. In fact, much to our delight, Columbia was in the midst of a very real urban renaissance.

It was quite clear that South Carolina's capital city had no intention of mimicking Atlanta, New York, or Los Angeles. Instead, there was a strong determination to embrace and amplify the best of the Midland's Southern traditions by blending its rich colonial past with its new contemporary flair. As each vision became a reality, the excitement and momentum continued to build.

Over the years, we've witnessed great positive change in Columbia. Our streets have become beautiful new cityscapes; a forgotten warehouse district has been reborn into the magnificent Congaree Vista brimming with great dining and shopping. Museums dot the area and offer everything from classical art to regional history. There are "First Thursdays" on a revitalized Main Street where Columbians and tourists have a chance to mingle with local artisans. And there are the eclectic sounds of jazz to

City of rivers, vistas, and dreams

Photo by Sam Holland

9

Photo by Brian Dressler

infuse the community with youth and joy. Every day, they join with students from 12 other colleges and campuses throughout the Midlands in both a celebration of learning and a strong commitment to innovation…and to having fun!

Before becoming a college president, my career was in public health, so it excites me to see our students and our Columbia neighbors enthusiastically engaged in so many outdoor activities. From jogging and biking along the scenic Riverwalk trails, to kayaking down one of our three rivers, or hiking through the ancient Congaree Swamp National Park, it's fair to conclude that Columbians are always on the move.

Since 1801, the University of South Carolina has played a significant role in the life of the Midlands. Today, its annual impact of more than $4 billion is felt statewide. Our Carnegie top-tier research university attracts renowned scholars from around the globe while Innovista draws budding entrepreneurs.

bluegrass to rock and even techno reverberating throughout the city.

In 2008, I became the 28th president of the state's flagship university and Patricia and I moved into the historic President's House on

USC's picturesque Horseshoe. Here, we have the distinct privilege of living among the 32,000 USC students who call Carolina and Columbia home. It is their enthusiasm and sense of discovery that continually

Photo by Stephanie Norwood

Our No. 1 ranked Darla Moore School of Business (DMSB) and its new home are a stunning addition to our West Campus and downtown Columbia! Beautifully designed by renowned architect Rafael Vinoly, the DMSB is on track to become the largest LEED Platinum building in South Carolina. Designed with our city and our planet in mind, it offers green rooftop terraces, the collection and reuse of rainwater and an abundant use of natural light for energy savings. The building's open and flexible design is sure to be a hub for community engagement. I am confident that the DMSB's new home will soon become a destination point for tourists nationwide.

Of course you can't talk about Columbia without talking about the mighty Gamecocks! In 2012, thousands of USC football fans streamed into the new Gamecock

Photo by Paul Ringger

City of rivers, vistas, and dreams

Photo by Stephanie Norwood

hotels and, of course, the nightlife is always jumping in Five Points after each game!

Another memorable grand opening came in 2009 when USC's Carolina Stadium became one of the premier ballparks in college baseball. Located in the West campus, it is home to one of the most dominant college baseball teams of the current era, with back-to-back national championships in 2010 and 2011 and a return to the finals in 2012. In fact, the entire West Campus is blooming and creating a new synergy with the city.

Today, all roads lead to Columbia. With three major interstates, I-20, I-26 and I-77 intersecting the city, and two major arteries, I -95 and I-85 just 90 minutes away, the city is a transportation crossroad.

Tourists and locals arrive daily to "zip the zoo" at the Riverbanks world-class zoo.

and gardens. Or they come to experience history, often stopping

Park where they cheered on the marching band, cheerleaders and football team as they marched down The Garnet Way into Williams-Brice Stadium. A Southeastern Conference favorite, Gamecock football has also had a substantial financial impact on the Midlands as each game brings in approximately $6.26 million. Fans are always welcomed with signature Southern hospitality at local restaurants and

to tour the State House, Governor's grounds and pre-Civil War homes. They come by planes, trains and cars to attend concerts at the Colonial Center, Koger Center for the Arts or Township Auditorium. They enjoy Shakespeare in the Park and local theater productions. And they come to sample our mustard-based barbecue and to enjoy some good shrimp and grits; the grits ground right here at the Adluh Flour Mill. In return, the Capital City also serves as a launching pad for day trips to Charleston, Greenville, Aiken, Myrtle Beach, Beaufort, and beyond. While it's always fun to go

away, it's even better to come back home. And if you're flying back in, surely there is no lovelier mid-sized airport than Columbia Metropolitan.

Is Columbia famously hot? Patricia and I think so. But come see

for yourself. "Hot" can mean many things to many people, but to me, it means "exciting" and "on the move."

HPastides

Photo by Helen Evans

City of rivers, vistas, and dreams

River City Dreams

Show me somebody who does not dream about the future and I'll show you someone who does not know where he is going. —Anonymous Adluh

From the beginning, dreamers shaped Columbia's future. The new capital would be in the state's center near three rivers. The city that was to be Columbia would be a river city. The dreamers who would come to this riverscape would shape the region in ways obvious and subtle with an influence felt beyond the city. Of course, some dreams were of little consequence, some iniquitous, and many were entertaining. Some proved monumental. Here are but a few.

General Robert E. Lee's Engineering Corps envisioned a waterpower facility where Saluda Dam stands today.

His vision was prophetic. The world's one-time largest earthen dam would stand there one day.

Secessionists dreamed of a new country.

Their dream became a nightmare when the deadliest war in the country's history resulted.

In 1898, a man contemplated a better way to organize documents.

Edwin G. Seibels' innovation changed the way people filed documents all over the world.

Photo by Helen Evans

City of rivers, vistas, and dreams

Did a Columbia boy by the name of Tommy dream of becoming president of the United States?

Whether the boy did or not, Thomas Woodrow Wilson made Columbia South Carolina's only presidential home site.

One hot night at Camp Jackson, two lieutenants walked back to their barrack discussing "a paper" they would establish.

TIME magazine resulted. Camp Jackson, known today as Fort Jackson, the U.S. Army's largest basic training facility, can boast it provided the genesis for TIME.

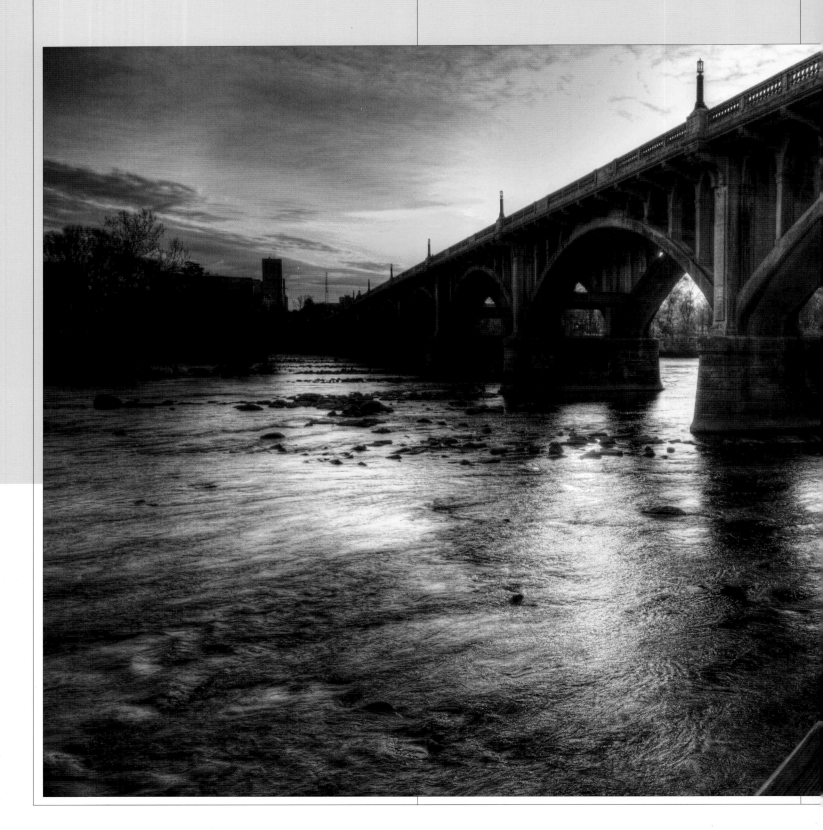

During World War II military strategists dreamed of a daring air raid on Tokyo, and the dream took shape here.

Colonel Jimmy Doolittle's daring raiders trained here in the Midlands. He and his men made the first attack on the Japanese mainland and, by design, crash-landed in China and the Soviet Union.

A Columbia woman shared Dr. Martin Luther King's dream and worked tirelessly to rid the land of the "separate-but-equal" doctrine.

The matriarch of South Carolina's Civil Rights movement, Modjeska Monteith Simkins, devoted her life to social reform.

DREAMS APLENTY HERE.

One might even say that people dreamed with their feet, sending their dance, the Big Apple, storming across the country.

The Shag would evolve from the Big Apple and become a South Carolina icon.

Local businessmen wished for a children's zoo with a nursery rhyme theme.

Today, Riverbanks Zoo & Garden ranks as South Carolina's number one attraction.

Conservationists dreamed of saving Congaree Swamp.

Their dream gave South Carolina its only national park.

Back in 1981, *Esquire* magazine published a series in which acclaimed writers penned essays on why they live where they live. Columbia resident, poet, and novelist, James Dickey, titled his "The Starry Place Between the Antlers."

"About halfway between the mountains and the ocean Columbia is hung up between two worlds of a distinction more than absolute, and is agreeably odd itself: a mixture of university town, southern political capital, and military base... Columbia is

Photo by Helen Evans

Photo courtesy of Christopher Dickey

GEORGIA-BORN JAMES DICKEY CLAIMED THAT HIS MOST IMPORTANT WORK WAS POETRY. *DELIVERANCE*, HIS ACCLAIMED NOVEL, BECAME A LANDMARK FILM THAT TURNED THE CHATTOOGA RIVER INTO LEGEND. A HIGHLY VISIBLE LITERARY FIGURE DURING THE LAST HALF OF THE CENTURY, HE CUT A WIDE SWATH THROUGH COLUMBIA. ▲

an easygoing place, with some fine old houses, good local theater, and the most imaginative small zoo I have seen ... But the best thing about Columbia is its meridional aspect: the way it balances Appalachia and the Atlantic."

Though Dickey was referring to shooting the stars with his sextant, let us construe Columbia's location on the 34th parallel as climactic balance. The Upcountry means cold winters and snow and the Lowcountry means tropical storms and hurricanes. Winters in the Midlands are mild.

Would it seem laughable if one described the climate here as dreamy?

The burning question is, "Just how much hotter is Columbia than its sister cities?" Weatherspark.com provides some statistics. Greenville's average temperature in July is 90. Charleston's is 90 and Columbia's is 91. Now what about that all-important humidity? In Columbia it ranges from a comfy 46 percent to a very humid 93 percent. Greenville's ranges from 36 percent to 89 percent. Charleston's ranges from 54 percent to 94 percent. All in all, not much difference, and that means people outside the region should refrain from bashing Columbia as too hot for comfort but bash they do.

WIS TV's General Manager Donita Todd addressed this bashing head-on. "For those of us who live here, Columbia seems to be coming of age. When *Charleston*

Post & Courier columnist Brian Hicks took umbrage with our city's accolades, many of you good citizens stuck up for your city!

We have a world-class art museum and zoo, performing arts, a vibrant downtown area, and charming neighborhoods. We have the State Capitol, USC, championship college sports, and beautiful natural resources that provide many enjoyable outdoor activities. It's a great place to be."

Co-author of *The Natural History of Congaree Swamp* Columbia native John Cely agrees with Todd. "I believe Columbia has really taken great strides in the past 30 years forging its own sense of identity and civic pride with the Vista and Three Rivers leading the way, along with such things as one of the best libraries for the size of the city anywhere, the art museum, the zoo, Lake Murray, and Congaree National Park."

It gets better... The Washington-based non-profit Partners for Livable Communities honors communities that develop themselves in the creative economy. Columbia made its list of 30 communities named "America's Most Livable Communities." ...and better. In July 2013, *Kiplinger Magazine* named Columbia one of "10 Great Cities to Live In." Columbia has also been named a top mid-sized market in the USA for relocating families for a basic reason: It is a family-friendly city. Just ask EDDIE, the world's largest boy who resides at EdVenture and calls Columbia home.

The fruit of dreams surround us... a wonderful zoo, parks, thriving enterprises,

> "The fruit of dreams surround us ..."

rehabilitated buildings, well-planned streets, greenspaces, historic homes, innovative technologies, diverse restaurants, and ruins that speak of past dreams. The list of good things can go on and on. Oh, sure there have been missteps such as 1970's Main Street's alien "monster" lights, but the theme of progress has been unabated. Planners and achievers' visions for the city and outlying areas have long shaped the future as others' aspirations preserve history and cultural resources while others harbor ambitions for conserving her natural resources. How many cities can claim to have a large forest in its limits, a national park at her fingertips, and three rivers running through her heart?

Main Street, once upon a time a bit rough around the edges, now enjoys a renaissance thanks to the combined efforts of art supporters and business. Check out First Thursdays when throngs of people walk Main Street to the accompaniment of music and good food and drink. Columbia and the Midlands, it should be said, assume a festive atmosphere throughout the year, not only on First Thursdays.

Yes, it gets hot here, but not much hotter than the sister cities. Why not turn a negative into a positive: we are "famously hot." Besides, in the extreme we have lakes and rivers to cool us. Columbia is a river city, and Columbians taking shelter here dream big. Columbia, city of rivers, vistas, and dreams is a place with a remarkable past and a future with promise—a place where great things have happened and will continue to happen.

Photo by Jay Browne

City of rivers, vistas, and dreams

19

Chapter 1

A City Rich in History & Geography

Photo by Jay Browne

RISEN FROM THE ASHES.

*T*he site that would become "Famously Hot" was crucial to South Carolina's development. The Congarees, a frontier fort on the Congaree River's west bank, represented the Santee River system's navigational limits. Being on the fall line, the fort signified the final point of upriver travel and the final area, too, where falling water could power mills. Rocks and gravity determined that people congregate there. As time passed, more people dwelled on the east side of the Congaree River. In 1754, this influx of people prompted the colonial government to establish a ferry to connect the fort with the growing settlements.

March 22, 1786, proved momentous. State Senator John Lewis Gervais of Ninety Six introduced a bill to create a new state capital, one to replace Charleston, one central to the state. The General Assembly chose Friday's Ferry on the Congaree's western side, according to David Brinkman, local historian and chair of the Greater Piedmont Chapter of the Explorers Club. The back-story behind the move was the growing numbers of backcountry residents, who by the late 1700s outnumbered Lowcountry dwellers four to one. The Lowcountry elites did not like the idea that "back woods" settlers might assume the Lowcountry's political power. To appease the back woods settlers,

Photo by Stephanie Norwood

A LANDMARK STANDS HERE. IN 1906, GUSTAF JONSON AND JOHANNES BENGSTON SYLVAN INSTALLED A FOUR-SIDED CLOCK ON THE SIDEWALK IN FRONT OF THEIR JEWELRY STORE. TWO SUCH CLOCKS ON MAIN STREET, EACH IDENTICAL, MAKE TIMELY LANDMARKS YOU COULD SAY. ▲

the General Assembly voted to move the state capital from Charleston to a tract of land along the banks of the Congaree near the confluence of the Broad and Saluda rivers.

Considerable debate attended the city's naming. One legislator wanted to call it "Washington," but the state Senate voted 11 to 7 to adopt "Columbia," a tip of the hat, some believed, to Christopher Columbus. Others said the name, "Columbia," was chosen because State Senator John Lewis Gervais dreamed that "the oppressed of every land might find refuge under the wings of Columbia." The General Assembly created the new capital on March 22, 1786.

One of the country's first planned cities, Columbia would sit 13 miles northwest of South Carolina's geographic center. John G.

Guignard laid out streets in a grid over a square two miles on each side. Streets paralleling the river took their name from Revolutionary War generals and heroes. Streets vertical to the river took their names from a variety of sources: location, the first President and his lady, agricultural products, and local luminaries.

> "The streets, by the way, are among some of the wider streets you'll find."

The streets, by the way, are among some of the wider streets you'll find. The perimeter streets and two through-streets were 150 feet wide. The remaining squares were divided by thoroughfares 100 feet wide. Why so wide? One myth of sorts holds that back then people believed mosquitoes could not fly more than 60 feet without dying of starvation.

Eli Whitney's cotton gin brought many a wagon down those broad streets, helping Columbia grow in the early 1800s from a frontier town into a market town. In 1820, South Carolina led the country in cotton production. Commerce drew people to a city in the making, and many discovered that summers here sizzle. As Wooley and Edgar wrote in *Columbia, Portrait of a City*, "More than one visitor compared a July or August visit in Columbia with a trip to India."

By the mid-nineteenth century Columbia consisted of about 6,000 people but a decade later, on the eve of the Civil War, Columbia ranked as the Carolinas' largest inland town. Lincoln's election prompted the South Carolina General Assembly to call a special convention to determine South Carolina's future as the Union went. The Seccession Convention opened December 17, 1860 in Columbia at the First Baptist Church. A smattering of smallpox cases broke out, so it is said, and the convention adjourned to Charleston. Three days later when South Carolina voted unanimously to leave the union, a party-like atmosphere enveloped Columbia. Down Charleston way, Confederate General P.G.T. Beauregard ordered Fort Sumter's shelling on April 12, 1861. The Civil War had arrived and near its end Columbia would burn, spawning one of the Civil War's most debated questions. Who burned Columbia?

This much we know. On February 17, 1865, General Sherman invaded Columbia. When Sherman departed, 84 of the city's 124 blocks had burned to the ground. Infamously hot you could say.

"It was a most fearful night. Not only the glare of the flames, but the millions of sparks and cinders that filled the air all helped to make an illumination that far surpassed the brightness of day. The storm of fire raged with unabated fury." —James Gibbes, from Frank Knapp's documentary, *Sherman's March: Final Revenge.*

"That long street of rich stores, the fine hotels, the courthouses, the extensive convent buildings, and last the old capitol, where the order of secession was passed, were all in one heap of unsightly ruins and rubbish." —David Conyngham, from *Sherman's March: Final Revenge.*

In *South Carolina, A History,* Walter Edgar wrote, "It was accepted as gospel that Sherman laid waste to Columbia and twenty-one other towns, but in reality his forces left a considerable number of antebellum buildings unharmed. For example, about two-thirds of the capital city's pre-Civil War structures remained after the state's first experiment with urban renewal."

Sherman, who claimed evacuating Confederates started the raging fires, later wrote: "Though I never ordered it and never wished it, I have never shed any tears over the event, because I

believe that it hastened what we all fought for, the end of the War." Belatedly, some Yankees helped fight the fires, but more than two-thirds of the city turned to ashes.

A neutral commission concluded that neither Federal nor Confederate officers intentionally or unintentionally burned the city.

Well over a century later Columbia is resurgent but some believe it suffers "sister" envy. Over a hundred miles to the south, onshore Atlantic winds refresh the church-steeple-rich "Holy City." Over ninety miles to the north, Greenville and its whitewater Falls Park rest in the Blue Ridge Mountain's cool shadows.

Situated between the tourist-pleasing Atlantic and the cooler mountains, Columbia, people claim bores and swelters. Thus, some say an inferiority complex dogs Columbia. John Cely acknowledged this sentiment. "Growing up here, it was not uncommon to hear folks say we were strategically located only a couple of hours from the mountains and the beach, but I don't think Greenville or Charleston ever thought of themselves as only two hours from Columbia. It was all implying that there were better things to do elsewhere."

At times it has seemed as if Columbia had to rely on antics to get attention. In the late 1970s the city erected tall streetlights on Main Street. People referred to them as

Columbia's First Baptist Church hosted the South Carolina Secession Convention December 17, 1860. The delegates drafted a resolution in favor of secession, 159–0.

Woodrow Wilson's parents built their home in Columbia in 1871, intending to live here. Though Dr. Joseph R. Wilson later moved his family to Wilmington, North Carolina, he and his wife rest eternally in Columbia's First Presbyterian Church.

Mayor William McB. Sloan and the aldermen of the city of Columbia established the Columbia Music Festival Association in 1897.

The Columbia Mills, first totally electric textile plant, opened in Columbia in 1893. The site for this hydroelectric-powered mill now houses the SC State Museum.

Edwin G. Seibels invented the vertical filing cabinet here in 1898, and file and document storage would never be the same.

Two lieutenants at Fort Jackson's predecessor, Camp Jackson, Briton Hadden and Henry Luce, walked back to their barrack discussing "a paper" they would found. From that discussion came TIME magazine.

When work ended on Lake Murray, it held the title of largest man-made lake in the world for power production. Dreher Shoals Dam reigned as the world's largest earthen dam.

Lt. Colonel Jimmy Doolittle and his pilots trained for the raid over Tokyo at what is now Columbia Metropolitan Airport.

In 1962, Johnny McCullough and Homer Fesperman wrote the music and Charles Weagly the lyrics for the SLINKY television commercial, the longest-running jingle in advertising history.

"monster" lights. Standing in the middle of Main the lights towered over the city like alien spacecraft. At 150-feet tall they called attention to themselves and destroyed the view of the capital at the south end of Main.

The true purpose of the lights was to cut down crime. Still... Mayor Kirkman Finley said, "It was apparent as soon as they went up they were a mistake from an aesthetic standpoint." It was a good day when they came down. Despite such blunders the city has its share of notable events.

RUINS & REMEMBRANCE

When history bequeaths ruins to a city, it blesses it with character. In the midst of Rome stand ruins aplenty. All too often we thoughtlessly destroy the old to make way for the new. Ruins stand in Columbia. In Riverbanks Zoo's Garden, you'll see the ruins of the old Saluda Mill and its lonesome but winsome keystone arch, monuments to Sherman's march through Columbia. You'll see, too, the old textile mill's granite blocks. Sherman burned the old mill itself.

In Columbia's Vista District, a unique ruin has taken on a series of lives. The Evans and Cogswell Company built the Confederate Printing Plant in 1864 for the manufacture of Confederate bonds and currency. In February 1865, when Sherman's army occupied Columbia, the building's contents were seized and the plant was burned. Sherman gladly burned it. Repaired in time after the war, the building was later used as a liquor warehouse for the South Carolina Dispensary System. Later rebuilt as a cotton-bale warehouse, it was reconceived through the inventive insight of the management of Publix as a supermarket in 2002.

The columned ruins of Millwood Plantation stand as remnants of a grand southern plantation that sat on 13,000 acres. Confederate General Wade Hampton III owned the plantation. The home burned February 17, 1865. All that remain are five large pillars and one pillar's stump. No proof exists that Sherman ordered the plantation's burning, but... he was passing through and Wade Hampton was a Confederate general. Do the math.

Fortunately, the city is blessed with fine homes from other eras, some of which were saved by visionaries.

HISTORIC HOMES—WHERE HISTORY LIVES

A city rich with historic homes shares a connection with its past, and keeps the past alive. Historic Columbia, a non-profit organization, does just that. It helps preserve Columbia and Richland County's historic and cultural heritage. Others as well have worked to preserve homes where history lives.

Hampton-Preston Mansion & Gardens. Ainsley Hall, a wealthy Columbia merchant, and his wife Sarah built this mansion in 1818. They sold the house in 1823 to Wade Hampton I, who updated the Federal-style home to Greek Revival. In the late 1830s, Mary Cantey Hampton and her daughter Caroline Hampton Preston enhanced the four-acre grounds turning the landscape into regionally acclaimed antebellum gardens, rich with native varieties and plants from around the world. The house

ALONG THE ZOO'S BOTANICAL GARDEN'S RIVER TRAIL, YOU'LL SEE THE OLD SALUDA RIVER FACTORY'S BEAUTIFUL STONE ARCH, MADE FROM GRANITE BLOCKS SPLIT ON-SITE. NEARBY OLD BRIDGE ABUTMENTS REMAIN AS WELL. ▼

Photos on this page by Paul Ringger

Photos on this page by Stephanie Norwood

passed through the Hampton and Preston families, who were forced to sell the estate after the Civil War. Home to four different colleges, it has served as a private residence, a governor's mansion, Union Army headquarters, a convent, educational institutions, and commercial space. Rehabilitated in the late 1960s, the historic mansion opened to the public in 1970.

Robert Mills House and Gardens. Ainsley and Sarah Hall hired Robert Mills to plan a Classical Revival townhouse. In time, the Presbyterian Synod of South Carolina and Georgia acquired it and established a seminary there. In 1960, the specter of demolition led to the eventual founding of

Historic Columbia. Spared the wrecking ball in 1961, the home underwent major restoration and opened in 1967 as an historic house museum. Only after Historic Columbia saved the property in 1960, did gardens come into play. Today, the garden blends an early 1970s landscape design, hallmarks of 19th century English-style gardens, and contemporary gardeners' features. One of only five National Historic Landmarks within Columbia, it is open for public tours.

Lace House. Thomas and Mary Caldwell Robertson, the youngest daughter of John Caldwell, lived in this antebellum home that retains its original intricate ironwork, ornamental

cornices, parquet floors, figured glass doors and brass chandeliers. It was built in 1854, a French architect responsible for its decidedly French style.

Mann-Simons Site. Formerly enslaved Charlestonians, Celia Mann, a midwife, and Ben Delane, a boatman, became the first generation of family members to live on this property. They laid a social and material foundation that let successive generations pursue various businesses and social undertakings. Although only one house stands today, the Mann-Simons Site was a collection of commercial and domestic spaces owned and operated by the same African-American family from at least 1843 until 1970. In

UNION FORCES COMMANDEERED THE HAMPTON-PRESTON MANSION AS HEADQUARTERS FOR GENERAL JOHN A. LOGAN. THREE OTHER HAMPTON FAMILY PLANTATIONS, HOWEVER, GOT THE TORCH. AN INTERESTING DETAIL: THE HAMPTON-PRESTON MANSION IS BUT HALF ITS SIZE AS THE BACK HALF OF THE MANSION WAS DESTROYED. ▲▲◄

HISTORIC COLUMBIA IS REVITALIZING THE GROUNDS TO INCLUDE A FOUNTAIN GARDEN AND A WELCOME GARDEN. ▲◄

ROBERT MILLS, THE WASHINGTON MONUMENT'S DESIGNER, CONCEIVED THIS CLASSICAL REVIVAL TOWNHOUSE IN 1823. IT WAS DECLARED A NATIONAL HISTORIC LANDMARK 150 YEARS LATER.. ▲▲

THE GARDENS SPLASH DOWNTOWN COLUMBIA WITH A SURPRISING GREEN SPACE. OLD TREES' SCARS TESTIFY TO THE PRUNING THEY'VE HAD, AND FLOWERING PLANTS BRING BLOSSOMS TO THE GROUNDS THROUGHOUT THE SEASONS. SEE OCCASIONAL BIG TENTS, TOO, FOR THE GROUNDS OFTEN HOST WEDDINGS. ▲

City of rivers, vistas, and dreams

Photo by Stephanie Norwood

Photo by Paul Ringger

SLAVE CELIA MANN, A MIDWIFE, SAVED HER MONEY AND PURCHASED HER FREEDOM AND, LATER, THIS HOME SOON AFTER IT WAS BUILT IN 1850. THREE BAPTIST CHURCHES TRACE THEIR ORIGINS TO SERVICES HELD IN HER HOME'S BASEMENT. ▲

THE ONLY HOME WILSON'S PARENTS OWNED, IT TELLS STORIES ABOUT THE WILSON'S LIFE AND RECONSTRUCTION THROUGH ITS MULTIMEDIA EXHIBITS, ARTIFACTS, AND DISPLAYS. THE HOME'S INTERIOR REFLECTS ITS DESIGN AS A TUSCAN VILLA. IT'S BELIEVED WILSON'S MOTHER PLANTED THE MAGNOLIAS ON THE GROUND. ▶▲

THIS ONE-TIME SHUL, SOLD AND CONVERTED INTO THE BIG APPLE NIGHT CLUB FOR BLACKS, STARTED THE BIG APPLE DANCE CRAZE IN 1937. ▶

1970, through eminent domain, the Columbia Housing Authority acquired the site, leading to a grassroots preservation movement that saved the main house, which opened as a museum in 1978.

Woodrow Wilson Family Home. This distinctive circa-1871 Italian villa-style residence was home to a 14-year-old boy named "Tommy." Since 1933 this property has operated as an historic house museum celebrating the life of Woodrow Wilson, the country's 28th president. Closed in 2005 due to structural issues, the Woodrow Wilson Family Home, the state's only presidential site, has undergone a multiphase, comprehensive rehabilitation. It reopened to the public February 15, 2014.

Modjeska Monteith Simkins House. Built between 1890 and 1895, this one-story Columbia Cottage was home to Modjeska Monteith Simkins, the matriarch of South Carolina's Civil Rights movement. This cottage provided lodging and meeting space for local and national civil rights leaders and NAACP lawyers such as

Thurgood Marshall. Simkins' most significant work was on the 1950 South Carolina Federal District Court case Briggs v. Elliott, a lawsuit that called for equalization of black Clarendon County Schools with white schools. Reworked in time, it was one of several cases challenging the "separate but equal" doctrine in the 1954 Supreme Court case Brown v. Board of Education. At this writing the house is not yet open for tours but is available for rentals.

Seibels House and Garden. The circa-1796 house blends architectural styles. Doric columns support a piazza stretching the home's entire length and dominate the front facade. Colonial Revival details embellish

the interior including molding and medallions. One of Columbia's most treasured buildings, the house was donated to Historic Columbia and adapted for offices and rental space.

The Big Apple. Originally built circa-1915 as the House of Peace synagogue, the building was sold in 1936 and reopened as the Big Apple Night Club, where the eponymous dance craze of that name swept the nation during the summer of 1937. Young blacks performed a group dance here there called the Big Apple. It attracted the attention of famed dance instructor Arthur Murray and songwriter Tommy Dorsey, who wrote "The Big Apple Swing." Abandoned in 1979,

Photo by Stephanie Norwood

WHEN SEGREGATION BARRED BLACKS FROM COLUMBIA HOTELS, CIVIL RIGHTS LEADERS SUCH AS THURGOOD MARSHALL STAYED IN THE MODJESKA MONTEITH SIMKINS HOUSE. ▲

the former club was moved three years later from its original location at 1138 Park to the corner of Hampton and Park Streets. The Big Apple was rehabilitated so as to preserve many of its original architectural features. Today its domed ceiling and neon moon and stars provide a beautiful rental venue for diverse events.

SANDHILLS, RIVER BOTTOMS, PIEDMONT, AND COASTAL PLAIN

Nature's bounties bless Columbia and the Midlands. Geographic provinces converge here. You'll find coastal plain, sandhills, river bottoms, and a touch of the piedmont here, as well as Broad River bluffs that conjure up the mountains. Riverbank trees dangling Spanish moss resurrect images of the Lowcountry. The region even hosts one of Earth's more mystifying landform—Carolina bays, "bays" because bay trees— magnolias and laurels— dominate them. At ground level they look like swamps. From above, they appear an elliptical with a northwest to southwest orientation that led many to believe a meteorite bombardment created them. (It didn't.) Exotic and beautiful, to explore a bay is a bit like an African safari. Rare plants and a rich diversity of wildlife live in bays. At the confluence of the Broad and Saluda, rare rocky shoals spider lilies cling to rocks, pleasing those who kayak past them.

Another of Columbia's distinctions is that whitewater runs through it. Walking the zoo's brick-paved bridge over the Saluda's last stretch, look upstream. Chances are good you'll see candy-colored kayaks heading your way. According to *American Whitewater* the kayakers find "cool routes and play spots" with names as colorful as the kayaks themselves like "Radio Tower, Stacy's Ledge, Maytag, Lap of Luxury, Mill Race, Cookie Monster, Blast'o Matic, and Pop Up Hole/Mosh Pit.

Eva Moore wrote in *Free Times*, "Right in downtown Columbia, the Lower Saluda and Broad Rivers come together to form the Congaree. These three rivers give the region an identity. And these aren't just any rivers, either, but wild, scenic rivers."

GREENWAYS & TREES

Many a city becomes not much more than a concrete canyon. Not Columbia. People dreamed of keeping Columbia and her region green, and their dreams are coming true. Parks aplenty splash greenery throughout Columbia and its outer reaches.

At 14 acres, Finlay Park is the largest and most visited park in downtown Columbia. Initially named Sidney Park, it was renamed for former Columbia mayor Kirkman Finlay. A waterfall cascades and spills into the park lake, echoing the nearby Saluda's whitewater upstream.

Memorial Park is a four-acre tract in the Congaree Vista between Main Street and the Congaree. This park provides a memorial to those who served their

THE SEIBELS HOUSE (PICTURED ABOVE AND BELOW), AN ARCHITECTURAL BEAUTY INSIDE AND LONG CELEBRATED FOR ITS GARDENS, RECEIVED FREQUENT MENTION IN 19TH- AND 20TH-CENTURY TRAVEL FEATURES.

Photos on this page by Stephanie Norwood

Photo by Bruce Flashnick

Photo by Bruce Flashnick

SPANISH MOSS IS NEITHER SPANISH NOR MOSS BUT FOR SURE IT BRINGS A TOUCH OF THE LOWCOUNTRY TO THE MIDLANDS AND ITS RIVER BLUFFS WHERE TREES DRIP WITH MOODY DRAPES OF GRAY. ▲

BLESSED BY THREE RIVERS, A NATIONAL PARK, AND A MAJOR STATE FOREST, COLUMBIA AND THE MIDLANDS ENJOY AN UNDERRATED WILDNESS. FLORA AND FAUNA SUCH AS GREAT EGRETS AND THE RARE ROCKY SHOALS SPIDER LILY FIND HABITAT HERE. WILDLIFE FINDS SUSTENANCE IN A REGION WHERE MAN AND WILDLIFE COEXIST.

WHITEWATER BRINGS BEAUTY AND RECREATION TO COLUMBIA ▶

country. The park was dedicated in November 1986 along with the unveiling of the South Carolina Vietnam Monument. In June 2000, the Korean War Memorial was dedicated there.

Granby Park opened in November 1998 as a gateway to the rivers of Columbia.

Granby is a 24-acre linear park with canoe access points, fishing spots, bridges, and a half-mile nature trail along the banks of the Congaree River.

> "Another of Columbia's rare distinctions is that whitewater runs through it."

The centerpiece of Martin Luther King Park is the bricked, circular, contemporary water fountain. An integral element of the park is the Stone of Hope monument. Upon the monument is inscribed a portion of King's 1964 Nobel Peace Prize acceptance speech: "History is cluttered with the wreckage of nations and individuals that pursued that self-defeating path of hate. Love is the key to the solutions of the problems of the world."

Riverfront Park runs beside the historic Columbia Canal and hosts a 2.5-mile trail. The park is popular for walking, running, bicycling, and fishing. Picnic tables and benches dot the walking trail. The park is part of the Palmetto Trail.

Sesquicentennial State Park, built by the Civilian Conservation Corps in the 1930s, has a beautiful 30-acre lake surrounded by trails and picnic areas. The park's proximity to downtown Columbia and three major interstate highways attracts local residents and travelers. The park also contains a two-story log house, dating back to the mid 18th century. Relocated to the park in 1969, it is likely the oldest building standing in Richland County.

Saluda Shoals Park reveals what rivers looked like before dams sprung up. Here, people observe nature, fish, kayak, jog, and bike. In older days a lot

Photos on this page by Paul Ringger

WATER FEATURES BRING BEAUTY TO THIS RIVER-CITY PARK AND THEIR WHITEWATER "WHITE NOISE" SOOTHES THOSE WHO COME TO FINLAY PARK, INCLUDING THOSE WITH DISABILITIES FOR IT IS ONE OF THE COUNTRY'S LARGEST HANDICAPPED-ACCESSIBLE PARKS. ▲

of hardworking farm families vacationed by the banks of shoals. Just 1.5 miles from the Dreher Shoals Dam, the Saluda runs free here.

The 350-acre park features an 11,000-square-foot Environmental Education Center, exhibit hall, auditorium, classrooms and a 3,776 square-foot outdoor deck. Miles of paved and unpaved trails provide wonderful places to walk and bike. Guided horse trails exist, too.

Proclaimed as one of the country's most promising ways to reconnect Americans to the natural world, the 9.5-mile Three Rivers Greenway is a growing park in Columbia, West Columbia, and Cayce. Riverfront pathways feature lighted trails and boardwalks, outdoor amphitheaters, restrooms and breathtaking views of the Columbia skyline in a dog friendly, ADA-accessible environment. People come to fish for stripers, watch birds, and relax. Ospreys fly against a city skyline. Parks abound in and around the city, including W. Gordon Belser Arboretum, Maxcy Gregg Park, Hyatt Park, Earlewood Park, Owens Field Park, and Southeast Park.

Things used to be different before the dreamers worked their magic. Prisoners at the old Columbia Correctional Institute used to shout at walkers and joggers. *South Carolina Wildlife* editor, David Lucas, remembers the old days before the Vista and Three Rivers. "The place was deserted and you could just walk in there, across the footbridge and wander through the waterworks buildings and along the canal. My wife remembers walking the old path along the canal in the shadow of the prison but prisoners would shout at her and others."

Today the prison's gone. It is a place where people experience serenity in the heart of the city—and no prisoners yell at them.

Dreamers at the Palmetto Conservation, a statewide non-profit conservation organization, imagined 500 miles of hiking and bicycling paths beside lakes, across mountain ridges, through forests, and into towns big and small. South Carolina's Palmetto Trail—the state's largest bicycle and pedestrian project—will run from the mountains to the sea. Its Capital City passage includes downtown Columbia's streets and sidewalks and the aforementioned Riverfront Park. In time, ambitious hikers and bikers will be able to go south from Columbia to the green Atlantic and north to the Great Blue Wall, the Blue Ridge escarpment.

Thanks to Harbison State Forest, Columbia can boast one of the largest public greenspaces inside a city's limits in the eastern United States. Here you can hike or bike 31 miles of roads and trails where the Catawba and Cherokee found sustenance in the woods and the Broad River. When European settlers arrived, an oft-used ford in the Broad River came to be known as Deutsche volk, known today as Dutch Fork. Here, a rocky ridge extends across the river, evidence of the Fall Line.

The Harbison Environmental Education Center, a 5,000-square-foot log building, serves as a classroom that teaches visitors about the forest, which consists of approximately 67 tree species.

Congaree National Park is the home of champions. That's how the National Park Service refers to the park, a jewel right in Columbia's back yard. In the park service's biological speak, "Astonishing biodiversity exists in Congaree National Park, the largest intact expanse of old growth bottomland hardwood forest remaining in the southeastern United States."

World-record trees live here where South Carolina's last virgin forest stands as tall as any temperate deciduous forest the world over. Congaree's trees have grown outward and upward, some for 800 years. Ninety protected tree species—half the number that all of Europe boasts—live here. Three-hundred-year-old loblolly pines, exceeding 15 feet in circumference and 150 feet tall, tower over the forest.

AN 800-FOOT, BRICK PEDESTRIAN BRIDGE ACROSS THE SALUDA RIVER CONNECTS RIVERBANKS ZOO WITH ITS BOTANICAL GARDEN ON THE WEST COLUMBIA SIDE. APPROXIMATELY 5,000 "TRIBUTE" BRICKS INSCRIBED WITH NAMES HONOR DONORS TO THE ZOO'S CAPITAL CAMPAIGN. VISITORS WALKING THE BRIDGE CROSS OVER WHERE SHERMAN'S TROOPS TRAVERSED THE RIVER IN FEBRUARY 1865 AFTER FIRING CANNONS UPON COLUMBIA FROM THE GARDEN'S SITE. ▼

Photos on pages 30-31 by Paul Ringger

City of rivers, vistas, and dreams

Photos on pages 32-33 by Bruce Flashnick

Nature set the country's 57th national park and South Carolina's first along the Congaree River's north bank some 20 miles southeast of Columbia. Walk the boardwalk over the blackwater. Take trails deep into the primeval forest. Canoe where otters braid through cypress knees. Inhale the same rich forest scents prehistoric foragers breathed.

In Lake Murray Country you see the fruits of dreams of damming mighty rivers for power. General Robert E. Lee's Engineering Corps first imagined a waterpower facility where Saluda Dam stands today. The Midland's signature lake takes its name from William S. Murray, an engineer involved in the dam's design and creation. Lexington Water Power

CONGAREE NATIONAL PARK AND LAKE MURRAY ENRICH THE MIDLANDS WITH NATURAL AND MAN-MADE BEAUTY. ONE—PROTECTED FROM MAN—AND ONE—CREATED BY MAN—OFFER WILDLIFE HOMES. THE LAKE, WITH ITS INUNDATED HOMES AND COMMUNITIES, HIDES MAN'S HABITAT FROM YESTERYEAR.

Company (South Carolina Electric and Gas) built the dam from 1927 through 1930.

BEYOND THE DREHER SHOALS DAM, BENEATH THE WATER, LIE OLD COMMUNITIES, A BRIDGE, RAILROAD CARS, AN OLD ROCK HOUSE, BOMB FRAGMENTS, AND B-25 BOMBERS. ▲

ELEVATED LANDS OVERLOOK SUBMERGED AREAS WHERE 2,000 MEN EARNED ABOUT 50¢ A DAY CLEARING 65,000 ACRES USING AXES AND CROSSCUT SAWS. ▲

MOONLIGHT MARLINS FLOCK TO THEIR BOMB ISLAND ROOSTS. ▲

AFTER A TWENTY-ONE-YEAR RUN, THE SOUTHERN PATRIOT RETIRED, NO LONGER OFFERING ITS POPULAR PURPLE MARTIN CRUISES, SPECIAL-EVENT CRUISES, OR COMPANY OUTINGS. ▲

Photos on pages 34-35 by Bill Barley

> "At completion, the lake's 1.6-mile dam was the world's largest earthen dam."

At completion, the lake's 1.6-mile dam was the world's largest earthen dam. Lake Murray, 41 miles long and 14 miles wide at its broadest, comprises approximately 50,000 acres of surface water and 520 miles of shoreline and reaches a maximum depth of about 200 feet. Located in the Piedmont, it covers parts of Lexington, Newberry, Richland, and Saluda Counties.

What's special about the lake is its wildlife habitat. Bald eagles and osprey hunt over the lake. Purple martins colonized Bomb Island, the United State's first purple martin sanctuary. When

> "Lake Murray... comprises 520 miles of shoreline and reaches a maximum depth of about 200 feet."

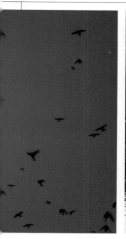

Canoe, kayaks, sail boats, pontoon boats, jet skis, speedboats, cabin cruisers, bass boats, and many others underscore the lake's reputation as a boaters' and fisherman's paradise. ▲

Competition is keen for shorefront property along the 691 miles of Columbia's watery playground. ▲

Intake towers—landmarks to boaters and drivers—stand 223 feet high, though water obscures much of the height. The four smaller towers funnel water to the penstocks. ▲

Colorful spinnakers use "green" energy to fly across Lake Murray, and big water regattas give sailing enthusiasts opportunities to display their talents. ▲

"What's special about the lake is its wildlife habitat. Bald eagles and osprey hunt over the lake."

do, abundant wildlife will remain, including wading birds such as the great blue heron.

birds roost in the summer months, no one is allowed on the island. People queue up in watercraft to watch the birds depart and return. When the birds leave in the morning, local weather radar reveals the image to be larger than 1989's Hurricane Hugo. At this writing it is possible the birds may be relocating approximately 40 miles to the north to Lake Monticello. Even if they

"Purple martins colonized Bomb Island, the United State's first purple martin sanctuary."

Chapter 2

A Burning Desire for Reinvention

CONGAREE VISTA

*L*incoln Street runs through the Congaree Vista. A historical marker at Gervais and Lincoln explains that Lincoln Street takes its name from Benjamin Lincoln, Revolutionary War hero. No way the capital of the state that first seceded would name anything after Abraham Lincoln.

Lincoln Street, bricked and cobblestone-like, feels a bit like Charleston. The Blue Marlin's signature shrimp and grits reinforce that impression. The restaurant sits where the old Seaboard Air Line Passenger Depot and Diner sat. That old diner—a scene right out of the 1940s—looked like an Edward Hopper painting. "Please pay when served" two signs over the counter insisted. From an old diner to the Blue Marlin, the restaurant provides evidence of the Congaree Vista's evolution where the past blends with the future. Here, you'll see rehabilitated fine old historic buildings, such as the Dupre Building at 807 Gervais Street. Thanks to a carefully planned rehabilitation it reflects its early 20th-century appearance even as it meets modern commercial and residential needs.

You'll see sparkling new structures, too. The Vista harbors a convention center and a Hilton with a Ruth's Chris Steakhouse. High-end

Photo by Paul Ringger

condos and townhomes, hotels, and mixed-use structures imbue the area with variety. Stroll through the Vista and you'll see art galleries, restaurants, shops, coffee bars, and businesses with surprising personalities. Down Gervais toward the Congaree River, for instance, the South Carolina State Museum and EdVenture Children's Museum draw residents and tourists. The first thing visitors walking into EdVenture see is EDDIE, the world's largest child. How big is he? Built from reinforced, molded plastic at 40 feet and 17.5 tons he's big enough for

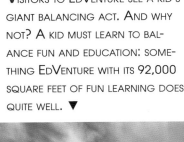

VISITORS TO EDVENTURE SEE A KID'S GIANT BALANCING ACT. AND WHY NOT? A KID MUST LEARN TO BALANCE FUN AND EDUCATION: SOMETHING EDVENTURE WITH ITS 92,000 SQUARE FEET OF FUN LEARNING DOES QUITE WELL. ▼

adults and children to climb into.

Up the street back toward the State House you'll see USC students walking to private student housing and residences in the Vista. Back down Huger over by the canal things sure have changed. It seems an eternity ago when the old CCI cast its foreboding shadow across the canal. Where the infamous electric chair, Old Sparky, formerly dispensed the ultimate form of justice, you'll now find residential units and access to Columbia's waterfront.

THE NEW MAIN STREET

Light post banners on old Richardson Street herald Columbia's "New Main Street," where a stroll makes for a cosmopolitan experience. Uptown on Main brings an eclectic mix to shopping. Here you'll find books, fashionable accessories, food, and gifts made in South Carolina. Main Street's First Thursday brings a carnival-like atmosphere to the street that once roared in flames. Live music, art, book signings, and street vendors serve food as people stroll from venue to venue. Main Street's First Thursday, a casual collaboration between Main Street merchants, began as an art show, which led to a monthly series of art shows with ever-increasing attendance. Many Main Street businesses joined in creating "an event for the people by the people" that brings exposure to Main Street's shops, art venues, and restaurants.

Drip brings a blend of Italian and Bohemian coffee shop traditions to Main. Don't be surprised to hear poetry readings and see rock documentaries at this coffee shop that specializes in pour-over coffee. Enjoy upscale breakfasts and lunches and surprising wines and beers such as Westbrook-One Claw of Mt. Pleasant and Foothills-Hoppyum of Chapel Hill.

Equitable Arcade, built in 1912, Columbia's first indoor shopping center, hosts artists, designers, and *Jasper* magazine, "the WORD on Columbia arts." Circa 1332 offers exclusive, handcrafted, must-have jeans, shirts, jackets, leather belts, and grooming supplies.

Across from the State House, The Oak Table brings regional dishes to a venue known for its progressive, palate-pleasing modern cuisine. Back up Main, the Nickelodeon, a non-profit theater overseen by the Columbia Film Society opened a new 99-seat theater on Main in 2012. Indie films and South Carolina-brewed Westbrook White Thai or IPA make a good tandem at "The Nick."

Wine Down on Main patrons bring take-out food, sip vino, and "picnic" in comfy suede chairs. This cozy wine bar features offbeat and traditional favorites, select beers, and complimentary hor d'oeuvres.

There's something for everyone on the New Main

Photo by Helen Evans

Photo by Stephanie Norwood

Main Street exhibits a more causal dress code these days. Where business once operated, people live a city lifestyle. The old Tapp's Department Store building hosts 42 elegant loft-style apartments with resident amenities such as free gym memberships. Private residences fill upper stories while art events take place in Tapp's Art Center for Visual and Performing Arts on the ground floor.

When SCANA, an energy-based holding company, relocated across the Congaree River to Cayce, it opened up new homes for as many as

IN THE PAST, THE EQUITABLE ARCADE BUILDING HOUSED A PRINT SHOP AND HAIR SALONS. TODAY IT IS HOME TO ARTISTS, AN ARTS MAGAZINE, AN UPSCALE CLOTHIER, AND GRAPHIC DESIGN STUDIOS. ORIGINALLY AN OPEN ARCADE, DESIGNERS MODELED IT AFTER ITALIAN MALLS. ◄

FESTIVALS DRAW THE CURIOUS AND ASSORTED VENDORS TO MAIN STREET THROUGHOUT THE YEAR. ▼

Photo by Paul Ringger

Street. The Whig, an underground bar with a retro feel, provides a favored gathering spot for the arts community and college students.

The Columbia Museum of Art has exhibited exciting works such as Annie Leibovitz's "Pilgrimage," subjects that weren't assignments but nonetheless of import to Leibovitz. As well, it houses a world-class collection of European and American fine and decorative art spanning centuries.

Revitalization efforts aim to re-establish Main Street

as a vibrant commercial and residential corridor, and the stretch of Main Street from Gervais to Blanding Streets has been streetscaped. Notable developments along Main Street include an 18-story, $60 million tower at Main and Gervais, the renovation of the 1441 Main Street office building as the new Midlands headquarters for Wells Fargo Bank, a new sanctuary for the Holy Trinity Greek Orthodox Church, and the Mast General Store in the historic Efird's Building.

City of rivers, vistas, and dreams

FIRST CITIZENS CAFÉ HOSTS BOOK SIGNINGS AND EVENTS IN THE BRENNEN BUILDING, A REHABILITATED MODEL FOR PRESERVATION. ▼

850 students and young professionals on Main Street. When USC is in session, students fill the sidewalks as they walk to the campus from The Hub at Columbia inside the old Palmetto Building.

A stroll toward the State House will take you to Bourbon, a great restaurant for Cajun and Creole dishes. If a type of bourbon is distributed in South Carolina, you'll find it at Bourbon in the Brennan Building, Main Street's oldest structure.

AN OLD BUILDING SPARKLES ANEW

The rehabilitated French-Victorian Brennen Building, circa 1870, on the 1200 block, has a unique story that began soon after the Civil War ended. Michael Brennen expanded his holdings, building a structure at the south end of old Richardson Street. Brennen died in May 1869 and never saw his building completed.

Over the decades the building's tenants sold books, clothing, candy, drugs, and liquor. The building housed showrooms, a garage, and offices for Columbia's first automobile dealerships—Etheredge Motor Company and Columbia Motor Company.

In 1891 Richardson Street became Main Street. From 1911 to 2002 the Brennen Building accommodated a legendary tenant, the Capitol Restaurant, which Columbians came to call the Capitol Café. It is said politicians made more than a few a political deals there.

After decades, the old eatery whose motto was "Our door is never closed" did, in fact, close. The café had seen its neighbor, the Columbia Opera House, give way to the Wade Hampton Hotel, which gave way to the high-rise now known as the Capitol Center. The building that long-housed the Capitol Café, however, did not give way. First Citizens acquired the Brennen Building in 2002 and, after deliberation,

Photo by Paul Ringger

decided to rehabilitate it. Many original architectural elements had survived and were painstakingly preserved, including much of the building's Main Street façade and the second floor's fireplaces and millwork. Today, the Brennen Building houses the First Citizens Café and office and meeting space for bank employees and clients while bringing new energy to the city.

John Sherrer, director of Cultural Resources for Historic Columbia Foundation, said, "Thanks to First Citizen's foresight and commitment to adaptively reusing the historic Brennen Building, Main Street's 1200 block features a wonderful juxtaposition of new and old architecture. Saving the Brennen Building as a venue for mixed-use applications paves the way for unique experiences on the capital city's Main Street and avoids the syndrome of cookie-cutter new development seen throughout the country."

NEW HIGH-RISES TOWER OVER MAIN

South Carolina's first "skyscraper" was the Barringer Building, a Georgian Revival structure built in 1903. In 1953, its name changed from the National Loan and Exchange Building to the Barringer Building. The Capitol Center, long known as the "AT&T Building," is the state's highest office building. (Taller manufacturing towers exist.) High-rise dreams keep raising downtown Columbia's skyline and name changes keep giving tall buildings new names. The Meridian

Building, a 17-story office tower, went up in 2004. First Citizens Bank completed its 170,000-square-foot, nine-story headquarters in 2006. The high-rises underscore Main Street's

ascension. Columbia-based writer, Dana Todd, wrote of the banks building on Main Street in *Columbia Business Monthly*. She tells a story of a bourgeoning financial center. Take the

THE PALMETTO BUILDING IS THE SITE OF THE SHERATON, A THREE-STAR HOTEL FEATURING ORIGINAL HARDWOOD FLOORING, ORNATE TILE MOSAICS, AND WOODWORK. ▼

Photo by Paul Ringger

Photo by Paul Ringer

new NBSC Building at 1221 Main Street. Bank Executive Vice President, Boyd Jones, said, "It's where business meets government—the most prominent position in the capital city. Fifteen years ago, businesses said no one would want to live on Main Street. Today, we have about 300 downtown residences that are on or touch Main Street with a 100 percent occupation rate. In the business improvement district surrounding Main Street, we have a large number of successful small business owners operating restaurants and retail establishments at both lunch and dinnertime."

Despite the recession, entrepreneurs and small businesses came to Main Street. "Banks follow business," says David Lockwood, senior vice president at Colliers International. "Having banks on Main Street is like the Good Housekeeping Seal of Approval, which facilitates more growth."

At Main Street's northern end, AgFirst Farm Credit Bank plans to buy and renovate the Bank of America Plaza. When AgFirst moves its 400 employees into the Class A office space, Main Street can boast one of the largest financial institutions in the state.

When you step back and take in Main Street's new high-rises and rejuvenated jewels like the Brennen Building and then see the throngs of people socializing, it's clear that Columbia's Main Street is poised for growth and eclectic prosperity.

BULL STREET DEVELOPMENT

Along Bull Street the former State Mental Hospital site will be developed as Columbia Common. The development, a 165-acre project in downtown Columbia, represents the largest and most consequential development in Columbia's modern history. A new residential complex along Calhoun Street, shops, and offices will bring a fresh aspect to downtown Columbia's personality. A minor league baseball stadium and team are part of the development as well. Thousands of new homes are expected to give the area a stable residential population.

RODNEY CARROLL CREATED APOLLO'S CASCADE, A COPPER-NICKEL, STAINLESS STEEL SCULPTURE THAT FRONTS THE COLUMBIA MUSEUM OF ART. ◄

FESTIVAL REVELERS ON MAIN STREET ENJOY THE SCULPTURE'S FOUNTAIN AND THE ICONIC MAIN STREET CLOCKS, MAIN STREET LANDMARKS. ▼

Photo by Paul Ringger

City of rivers, vistas, and dreams

W.B. SMITH WHALEY NEVER COULD HAVE DREAMED HIS OLYMPIA MILL WOULD EVENTUALLY PROVIDE RESIDENTIAL ACCOMMODATIONS. WHALEY NAMED THE MILL AFTER ADMIRAL DEWEY'S FLAGSHIP, THE OLYMPIA. THE OLD MILL WAS COMPRISED OF A COMPLEX OF BUILDINGS.

The State Mental Hospital complex is known for its historical architecture. Much of it will be reclaimed, adding to the site's authenticity.

The development of a park featuring a creek, pond, jogging trails, and dog park bring a green space element to the development, which holds the potential to dramatically elevate Columbia's presence as a city of parks. With its hotel and conference space, the development promises to give Columbia a new gathering place. The development holds the potential to magnify Columbia's nascent, urbane feel.

OLD NEIGHBORHOODS'

NEWFOUND GLORY

No city is immune to aging and often the old neighborhoods reveal aging the most. Fortunately, a fountain of youth exists— historic preservation. Neighborhood associations throughout Columbia have had the vision to establish guidelines for keeping their homes and streets graceful and historic. Preserved neighborhoods balance the city's more contemporary elements and provide pleasant places to live. These stately old neighborhoods have something many newer neighborhoods covet: gorgeous old oaks, historic architectures, spacious yards, and a connection to the past.

The concept of a New South was cultivated after the Civil War reaching its height before 1910. It was aimed at making the region less dependent on agriculture through economic progress, emphasized civic duty, and accepted social changes. Determined not to depend on the North for textiles, the South set about building textile mills—mill villages sprang up. By the late nineteenth century, steam and electrical power freed mills of their dependence on rivers. Manufacturers could build a mill anywhere.

By 1907, six mills hummed in Columbia: Richland, Granby, Olympia, Capital City, Columbia, and

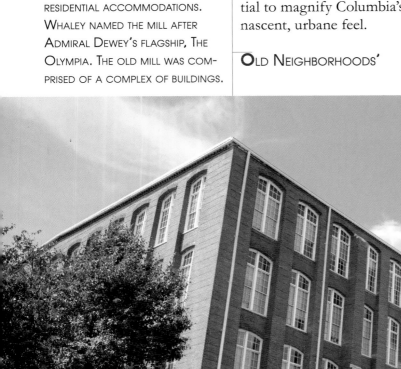

Photos on pages 44-45 by Paul Ringger

Palmetto. The Olympia Mill opened in 1899. With over 100,000 spindles and 2,250 looms, it was the largest cotton mill under one roof in the world. Located next to the Granby Mill, the original Olympia site covered 104 acres. The State newspaper waxed poetic about Olympia in 1901, heralding it as "Peerless Olympia, Wonderful Example of Engineering Skill," proclaiming it "the most beautiful, the most majestic, and upon close investigation, the most admirable specimen of mechanical construction in the realm of Southern industrial activity."

One of South Carolina's more architecturally outstanding early twentieth century industrial buildings, the mill features distinctive, soaring twin towers. If you are in one of Columbia's high-rise buildings and look south, you will see those gleaming copper-clad towers.

You cannot miss the mill village with its simple frame dwellings and state-named streets. Olympia Mills Village and its community live on with renewed purpose. The old mill, now converted to apartments, attracts USC students who enjoy living close to the university, Williams-Brice Stadium, and Carolina Stadium (a state-of-the-art baseball stadium). Come football season, tailgaters gather along the state-named streets and do their part to make sure the "Gamecocks are playing and the Brice is swaying."

Named for its old cotton warehouses, the Cottontown/Bellevue neighborhood was listed on the National Register of Historic Places in 1997 and designated a local Architectural Conservation District in 2009. Cottontown's Neighborhood Association formed a Historic Preservation Committee, which raised awareness of historic, architectural, and archaeological resources worthy of historic preservation.

In 1896, when a pavilion and casino transformed areas

WHAT WAS REPORTED AS "THE LARGEST COTTON MILL UNDER ONE ROOF IN THE WORLD" IN 1899, OLYMPIA CONSISTED OF A LARGE FOUR-STORY, RED BRICK MAIN MILL BUILDING AND A TWO-STORY RED BRICK POWER PLANT. OTHER BUILDINGS INCLUDED A ONE-STORY BRICK POWER PLANT, A STORAGE BUILDING, AND TWO SMALL BRICK GATEHOUSES.

north of the city, Cottontown desired a name with a bit more polish. "Bellevue Springs" fit the bill. Bellevue played an important role in the early expansion of the capital city. Most of its homes were built between 1925 and 1940. Today, it is an intact example of one of Columbia's earliest planned suburban residential neighborhoods.

The historic suburb of Melrose Heights/Oak Lawn developed in the early twentieth century. You'll find the Melrose Heights/Oak Lawn Historic District at the fork of Millwood Avenue (historically known as Garner's Ferry Road) and Gervais Street (along with its extension, Trenholm Road). Founded in 1900, this quaint neighborhood sits just five minutes from downtown. In 2003, the community voted to designate the neighborhood as an architectural

conservation district. Residents love their gardens and eclectic homes. Here you'll find homes featuring Tudor Revival, Craftsman, Colonial Revival, and Prairie styles. You'll also find vernacular homes, '40s brick cottages, and kit houses people ordered from Sears— the ultimate DIY project. While most houses date to the 20s and 30s, many houses in the neighborhood reflect the building boom that occurred in Columbia just after World War II. *This Old House* magazine named the neighborhood one of the best places in the country to buy an old home.

Popular Elmwood Park retains its historic character as a turn-of-the-century neighborhood. Most of the neighborhood had been a racetrack and fairground until 1903. Its architecture includes Queen Anne, Four-Square, Colonial Revival,

and Craftsman-influenced bungalows. Several shotgun houses stand in the earliest developed part of the neighborhood. Two historic schools are located there, the still-functioning Logan Elementary and the former Wardlaw Junior High, now a residential senior facility known as Wardlaw Apartments. The neighborhood was listed in the National Register of Historic Places in 1991 and designated a local Architectural Conservation District in 1988.

Like other older neighborhoods, Old Shandon/Lower Waverly neighborhood developed as an early suburb. In the 1890s, some viewed it as the city's first real suburb. When the city's new electric streetcar lines arrived in the early 1900s, construction accelerated. Old Shandon Historic District was listed in the National Register of Historic Places in 2003 and

was designated a local Protection Area in 2001. Among its general protection guidelines you'll find this: "The main strength of this predominantly residential Historic Protection Area is the harmonious way that many diverse housing styles fit together to create a pleasant living environment." It is a highly desirable place to live, especially among the younger professional set.

The Granby Mill Village is perhaps the best collection of mill housing in South Carolina, a fine example of late nineteenth century mill village design. The neighborhood's connection with textile mill designer W.B. Smith Whaley gives it historical importance. Whaley was one of South Carolina's more prominent textile industry figures. Here you will see "saltbox" style houses built from 1897 to 1899. Here, too, you'll find a translation of a traditional New England Mill Village in a late nineteenth century southern setting. The neighborhood was listed in the National Register of Historic Places in 1993 and designated a local Architectural Conservation District in 2010.

The Earlewood neighborhood melded several subdivisions that developed after 1900 and achieved one identity. This early neighborhood developed from a time of great suburban expansion in the early twentieth century through post-World War II's housing boom. In the neighborhood's Area A, many historic structures were built between 1910 and 1945 while in Area B, development occurred between 1940 and 1955. Designated a local Protection Area in 2005, the neighborhood describes itself as tranquil and is not far from downtown and urban amenities.

Location has long made Wales Garden a popular neighborhood. Just ask the many joggers and bikers plying its streets and sidewalks. This neighborhood's beautiful homes and gardens and close proximity to USC, the State House, and Fort Jackson enhance its appeal.

Edwin Wales Robertson developed Wales Garden between 1915 and the early 1940s. Wales, a businessman and president of the Columbia Electric Street Railway, Light & Power Company, made sure Wales Garden had excellent public transportation. Today Wales Garden remains attractive and stable. The neighborhood was designated a local Architectural Conservation District in 2008.

MOVEMENTS TO PRESERVE HOMES WITH CLASSIC ARCHITECTURAL BLOODLINES PROVE POPULAR IN RESURGENT NEIGHBORHOODS FRINGING THE CITY.

WHAT'S OLD POSSESSES NEW APPEAL TO YOUNG COUPLES AND FAMILIES WHO FIND THE COMBINATION OF CHARM, HISTORY, AND PROXIMITY TO THE CITY HARD TO RESIST.

Photos on pages 46-47 by Paul Ringger

City of rivers, vistas, and dreams

Chapter 3

All Routes Lead To Columbia

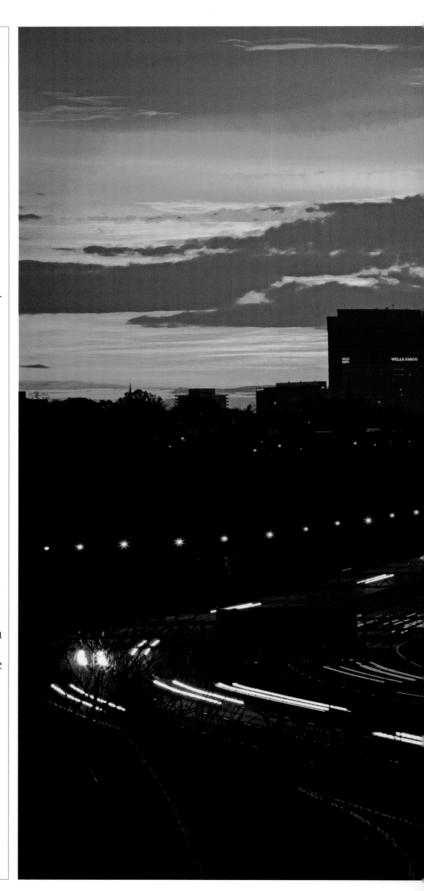

By land, air, and rail they come and go. Columbia, city of three rivers, enjoys three avenues of transit—by land, by air, and by rail. Interstate 26's extension, I-126, shoots into the heart of the city. As the city skyline comes into view, you see the white, frothy Saluda River rapids to your right. In the summer, you get an extra treat: crepe myrtles and magnolias. Lavender and white myrtles give the median near the Huger/Elmwood Street split color, and preceding the split, magnolias flaunt cream-colored blossoms, reminders that Columbia is a city of the subtropics.

BY LAND...

Columbia is a city of interstates, too. A glance at a map reveals that getting to Columbia is fairly easy thanks to the dreams of a World War II general who had seen Germany's Autobahn. In the early 1950s, President Eisenhower, a general to the end, envisioned "broad ribbons" laden with tanks and troops, and South Carolina got its share of what became the interstate highway system. Today, a grid of steel, cement, and asphalt makes it possible to cross South Carolina and get to Columbia pronto. Columbia is highly accessible with Interstates 20, 77, and 26 running through it. Not that many cities have three interstates, and if you

Photo by Jay Browne

glance at that map again, you'll see that I-95 and I-85 are short drives away.

Farther away, but within reasonable driving distance, are interstates that connect spider-web-like with interstates that lead to Columbia such as I-40, I-74, and I-16. Yes, getting here from most anywhere is easy.

BY AIR...

World War II changed the land and skies over metropolitan Columbia. Around 1941, the United States War Department acquired the nearby Lexington County Airport and expanded it, building runways, hangars, roads, buildings, and other facilities.

In February 1942, Jimmy Doolittle arrived in Columbia and called for volunteers for a secret military mission —the famous April 18, 1942, Doolittle Raid over Tokyo. At this time Columbia's Owens Field was handling air traffic. The City of Columbia built a new terminal at the Lexington County Airport in the early 1950s, which burned, but was quickly replaced and used until the present terminal opened in 1965 and updated in 1997.

Today's Columbia Metropolitan Airport far exceeds the dreams of early aviation pioneers who established it in the early 1940s. From the old Lexington County Airport, Columbia Metropolitan Airport (CAE) grew into a 2,600-acre city. Each year, the airport serves more than 1.2 million passengers and processes more than 168,000 tons of air cargo.

BY RAIL...

The Amtrak station used to sit on Lincoln Street, now home to the Blue Marlin. Back then, after midnight, Amtrak's Silver Star, an assemblage of rolling steel, would pull out of Lincoln Street and creep through town. It eased past a building where the word *Adluh*

Photo by Brian Dressler

Photo by Sam Holland

glowed red, a place where men milled flour and corn-meal, occasionally giving away free biscuits on city mornings. An inexorable pressure built, and soon city lights were no more as passengers were spirited past Columbiea, south to Florida.

Visions of change arrived and the old red brick Seaboard Air Line and Amtrak station (1903) at Gervais and Lincoln was abandoned and then restored. It has been the Blue Marlin Restaurant ever since.

The Amtrak station moved to 850 Pulaski Street when the city removed the rails and Seaboard Air Line Railway trestle along Lincoln Street. The Silver Star still rolls into Columbia, as part of its run from New York City south to Miami, Florida with connections to many other cities including Washington, DC, Richmond, Raleigh, and points beyond. The Silver Star shares much of its track with the Silver Meteor. Amtrak provides ticketing and baggage services in Columbia, served by two daily trains.

THE PHRASE, "YOU CAN'T GET THERE FROM HERE," WILL NEVER APPLY TO THE CAPITAL CITY. COLUMBIA'S CENTRAL LOCATION HOSTS A HUB FOR A NETWORK OF TRANSPORTATION INFRASTRUCTURES. GETTING AROUND, INTO, AND OUT OF COLUMBIA IS EASY; GREATLY BENEFITTING COMMERCE AND TOURISM ALSO BENEFIT.

AS IN MANY CITIES, YOU'LL SEE FREEWAY TRAFFIC, PASSENGER AND FREIGHT TRAINS, AND COMMERCIAL AIRLINERS—OFTEN AT ONE TIME. THE SUNBELT IS A REGION ON THE GO AND COLUMBIA DOES ITS PART TO KEEP PEOPLE COMING AND GOING.

Photos on this page by Tom Poland

City of rivers, vistas, and dreams

Chapter 4

A Lifestyle To Relish

Photo by Helen Evans

Life in the sunbelt is good. Columbia owes its "Famously Hot" reputation to its planetary address: 34.0008° N, 81.0353° W. That places it on the 34th parallel—the subtropics. You'll find some of the world's greenest and most luxurious places along this parallel. Columbia is in a region where, historically, rain comes often. Evenings bring out the katydids, tree frogs, and cicadas, singing their glorious rain songs. Many wildlife species will tell you life outdoors is good here. As you'd expect, the region makes a great setting for festivals and a wholesome lifestyle. Here, then, are some of the many festivals taking place in Columbia and the Midlands.

Fun, Festivals, & Family

Throughout the year, festivals draw families, residents, and visitors to Columbia and the Midlands. Owing to summer's temperatures many festivals take place in May and October. Festivals with strong seasonal ties take place in the appropriate season.

Calhoun County's Purple Martin Festival started in the fall of 1969 when the film, "The Griggsville Story" was shown at the St. Matthews Rotary Club. Griggsville, a small town in

ALL WORK AND NO PLAY MAKES FOR A DULL LIFE BUT THAT'S NOT THE CASE THROUGHOUT THE MIDLANDS WHERE FESTIVALS CELEBRATE MAN'S CONNECTION WITH THE EARTH, NATURE, HERITAGE, AND COMMUNITY. IN COLUMBIA AND ALL ACROSS THE MIDLANDS, ANNUAL FESTIVALS DRAW BIG CROWDS. A BIT OF INTELLECTUAL CELEBRATION TAKES PLACE IN COLUMBIA, "BETWEEN THE EARS", YOU COULD SAY. THE SC BOOK FESTIVAL BRINGS BOOKLOVERS OUT IN DROVES.

FROM PEACHES AND IRISES TO PATRON SAINTS, FESTIVALS GIVE PEOPLE A REASON TO MINGLE ALL AROUND THE MIDLANDS.

southwestern Illinois, was experiencing unpleasant summers due to mosquitoes and other insects. In their efforts to find solutions it was suggested they attracted mosquito-eating purple martins to Griggsville. The birds reduced the population of insects in the area. When scheduled, the festival takes place in April.

In Fairfield County in May the Wings and Wheels Air Festival offers people the chance to see helicopters and fixed wing aircraft up close at the Fairfield County Airport.

In May, the Orangeburg County Chamber of Commerce and City of Orangeburg hold the Annual Orangeburg Festival of Roses. This event celebrates the blooming of roses and the beginning of a yearlong opportunity to enjoy the Edisto Memorial Gardens along the banks of the

Edisto, the world's longest black water river.

Sumter's Iris Festival is South Carolina's oldest continuous festival. The three-day festival in May includes concerts, an arts and crafts show, a flower show, a quilt show, car shows, contests, and children's activities. The fun begins the evening before the festival, with the annual Crowning of The King & Queen followed by the Taste at the Gardens, featuring great music and savory

offerings from some of the area's leading restaurants and caterers.

Gilbert hosts the Lexington County Peach Festival every year on July 4th (July 3rd if the 4th falls on a Sunday) at the Gilbert Community Park. Festivities kick off with a parade and continue until 10:00 pm when fireworks close the festival with a bang.

Ridge Spring's Harvest Festival began as the Centennial Celebration on October 30, 1982, with a theme of "Reunion on the Ridge." Each year since, family and friends return to capture the spirit of fun and small-town living. The Harvest Festival always takes place on the fourth Saturday in October.

The Fine Arts Center of Kershaw County's Carolina Downhome Blues Festival brings international musical talent to downtown Camden. Over 40 performances take place at 16 different sites. With blues for all tastes from classic soul to horn-driven funk to blues-rock to the best of acoustic blues, the music suits many. The festival takes place the first full weekend in October.

COLUMBIA FESTIVALS

Throughout the year, families find fun things to do at Columbia's various festivals.

Each March the St. Patrick's Day Festival in Five Points attracts revelers eager for fun and an early spring. Live bands, arts and crafts, food, and more attract a

Photo courtesy of the Peach Festival

Photo by John Mann, courtesy of St. Pat's in Five Points

huge crowd. It is the Midlands biggest, annual street festival and one of the Southeast's largest St. Patrick's Day celebrations. Over 40,000 people flock to Five Points, a popular college student venue, to celebrate all things green and Gaelic, welcome the arrival of spring, and promote businesses in the Five Points village.

The Columbia International Festival is a two-day celebration of the music, culture, foods and performing arts of South Carolina's diverse cultures, nationalities, races, and language groups. Residents and visitors alike come to come to see, taste, learn, and enjoy all that gives the Midlands an international flavor. Each year features a different international focus.

Eau Claire Fest is a day-long April festival that celebrates the very best of this North Columbia community. It features a 5K run, the Fonky Fest Parade, good food, cowboys riding and roping, and more.

Indie Grits Festival, established in 2007, began as an independent film festival for Southeastern filmmakers. This April festival also features music, art, food, performing art, and technology. The Nickelodeon Theater hosts it annually. Festival organizers' dreams and visions sought to break down the walls intimidating Southern media makers by creating exhibition opportunities for work often overlooked elsewhere. Indie Grits showcases the city's very best culinary, theatrical, artistic, and musical talent.

Artista Vista grew from a minor studio showcase in the early 1990s into Columbia's oldest and most celebrated gallery crawl. This April festival draws artists and collectors alike. While local artists provide most exhibits, works come from as far away as Japan, Romania, and Poland. Join in; the three-day event offers something for everyone. Galleries will host visitors and offer complimentary beverages and hors d'oeuvres, and some will also present live entertainment to make this a truly well-rounded event. Additionally, enjoy pop-up installation art, music and other entertainment spread throughout the Vista.

Photo courtesy of the Indie Grits Festival

PICK A MONTH AND YOU'LL FIND
MORE THAN A FEW FESTIVALS
PLANNED. FROM THE NOTES OF
BOLD AND SPIRITED PLAYERS OF
GRAND PIANOS TO HOMEGROWN,
SUN-RIPENED TOMATOES, COLORFUL
CHARACTERS, AND TRADITIONAL
DANCES, VARIOUS FESTIVALS FILL
MANY WEEKENDS. NOW AND THEN A
FESTIVAL RUNS ITS COURSE BUT A NEW
ONE WILL EMERGE.

Since its debut in the spring of 1997, the SC Book Festival has grown in size and consequence, becoming a nationally recognized and regionally dominant literary festival. Visionary organizations such as the South Carolina Arts Commission and the Humanities Council laid the foundation for the festival. Over the years, writers such as Jack Bass, Robert Olen Butler, Dottie Benton Frank, Gail Godwin, Josephine Humphreys, Reynolds Price, and Mickey Spillane have made the festival more and more popular. Today, writers such as Pat Conroy and Ron Rash draw book lovers to the Columbia Metropolitan Convention Center for this much-anticipated event in May.

Each June, the Southeastern Piano Festival transforms the University of South Carolina School of Music and Columbia into a major cultural destination. Audiences and young piano talent come from across the United States. The festival presents a perfect symbiosis of the new generation of pianists in search of inspiration and challenge and the world-class guest artists who provide that inspiration. Whether one is a budding piano virtuoso, an educator, or a music aficionado, the festival offers something for everyone who loves piano.

Each Saturday during summer months, people bring picnic baskets and lawn chairs to Finlay Park

Photo courtesy of Tasty Tomato Festival

for a free concert including blues, rock, beach, jazz, big band and more. Throughout the summer, music lovers of many genres find delight in the free concerts.

"City Roots, Your In-Town Sustainable Farm" hosts the Tasty Tomato Festival each July. Presented

Photo Courtesy of Southeastern Piano Festival

by Sustainable Midlands, an organization that advocates, educates, and celebrates solutions that balance the needs of the community, the environment, and the economy, the Palmetto Tasty Tomato Festival celebrates locally grown food, its growers, restaurants that serve it, markets that sell it, and the people who eat it. Tasty Tomato's programming includes a free heirloom tomato tasting, live music, local food and drink vendors, tomato bobbing, and the highly anticipated Tasty Tomato Contests.

Jubilee: Festival of Heritage celebrates the rich cultural heritage and entrepreneurial spirit of a local family. The Jubilee:

Festival of Heritage takes place each year in August on the grounds of the historic Mann-Simons Site. Jubilee activities include hands-on demonstrations from some of the region's most skilled artists and craftsmen, musical entertainment including African drumming, R&B, jazz, and gospel, and vendors with African-influenced and traditional merchandise.

The four-day Greek Festival, held annually in September at the Holy Trinity Greek Orthodox Church, celebrates Orthodox Faith and features traditional Greek dances, ceremonies, music, theatre, food, and beverages. It provides the opportunity to experience the history of Greece.

Irmo's Okra Strut, a September festival, grew from a dream and an anecdote to become a popular festival. The Lake Murray-Irmo Woman's Club needed a way to raise money for a new library. About that time Gene McKay, a morning radio show personality, pondered

MANY FESTIVALS RAISE MONEY FOR A VARIETY OF WORTHY EFFORTS. GOOD TIMES, GOOD FOOD, AND GOOD CAUSES ATTRACT GOOD CROWDS THROUGHOUT THE YEAR ALL ACROSS THE MIDLANDS.

Photo Courtesy of Columbia Greek Festival

the name of an Irmo hardware store, "The Ancient Irmese General Store."

"What were these Ancient Irmese like," wondered the late McKay. "Probably short people—a farming tribe who lived off okra!" The club had its name and the rest is history. The two-day festival, which takes place during the last weekend in September, features a street dance, 10 K road race, golf tournament, arts and crafts, rides, food, and South Carolina's largest festival parade.

Viva La Vista, a September, "wallet-friendly" food festival in the heart of the Congaree Vista, covers close to four city blocks. Live music, beverages, and a taste of the Vista's most popular restaurants? They are all here in a great family event.

In October, the Jam Room Music Festival, the first and only music festival of its kind in Columbia, rocks revitalized Main Street with an eclectic musical lineup on two stages. The festival of late has teamed up with the American Diabetes Association. Festival Director of Marketing, Linda Toro, said, "We're doing a 25-mile training ride for the Tour De Cure on the day of the festival. The actual Tour De Cure happens in the spring." The festival's Tour De Cure component brings cyclists together for a good cause—seeking a cure for diabetes.

The South Carolina State Fair takes place each October. Rides, food, concerts, games, and racing attract people from far and wide. Exhibits featuring art, crafts, flowers, and livestock cover the fairgrounds. The Ferris wheel, seen from afar, makes it colorfully clear that the fair is in town.

Vista Lights, held each year in mid-November, is an open-house walking tour and reception with entertainment by local musicians and carriage rides through Columbia's antique district.

Crafty Feast, a December indie craft fair, brings 100-percent handmade, juried, independent craft

Photos on this page by Tom Poland

Spicy Hot & Simmering

Restaurateurs bring culinary dreams to life here. No matter the consideration—location, price range, cuisine, local eateries, franchises, or unique cafes—Columbia's restaurants will please your tastes. You'll find fare and culinary influences from around the word here. Of course, the staples of the South, southern fried chicken and BBQ, thrive here.

Restaurant names alone prove enticing. Some use intriguing numbers: **2 Fat 2 Fly, 32° A Yogurt Bar, and Burger Tavern 77**. Some names hint at what to expect: **Gervais & Vine**. Others use exotic names ... **Terra and Solstice Kitchen**. Some use initials such as **M Café**, while some burst with creativity such as **Higher Grounds Books & Beans** and a somewhat Bohemian restaurant, **Café Strudel**. Some make you scratch your head such as **Carolina Strip Club** (a steakhouse).

California Dreaming serves excellent salads and steaks and seafood in the historic old Union Train station, gloriously saved from the wrecking ball. Built in 1902, it housed the Southern Railway and Atlantic Coast Line. Inspired by sixteenth century English manor house designs, the stepped gables, brick and stone, and towering chimneys place the building within the mainstream of Jacobethan Revival architecture in America. You'll love its architecture, high ceilings and beams, and food.

Gervais & Vine, a Spanish-styled tapas bar, brims with Mediterranean culinary influences. It is a great place to convene before or after special events. Enjoy top-shelf spirits and a good selection of craft beers.

Ruth's Chris Steak House brings its long and delicious history to the Vista. Over four decades ago, Ruth Fertel, a divorced mother of two, mortgaged her home for $22,000 to buy a small 60-seat restaurant in New Orleans named Chris Steak House. Shortly thereafter, a fire forced her to change location and she renamed the restaurant, "Ruth's Chris Steak House."

In northeast Columbia **Solstice Kitchen & Wine Bar** pleases patrons with its "New American" cuisine. In its own words: "As the seasons change, so does Solstice. Please come experience the changes with us!"

With its book-lined shelves, the **Thirsty Fellow**, in the USC Innovista, evokes images of a cozy library where one can dine and enjoy adult beverages. Its atmosphere never disappoints and the fish and chips please many. From students to businessmen, an eclectic clientele comes here with a thirst and an appetite.

DiPrato's Delicatessen offers patrons friendly service and a pleasant, neighborly feeling. You could say a Southern breeze laden with Italian accents drifts through this New York-style delicatessen. From the start, the culinary chemistry between Dianne Light and Bill Prato sparkled. As the accolades poured in, a dream stirred within Bill: giving Columbia a *true* deli experience.

The Blue Marlin on Lincoln Street gives you a Charleston-like feeling, and with good reason. Besides the cobblestone street running along side it, legend glorifies it as a place where "the aroma of Low Country flavors coming out from the back kitchens could not be ignored."

In Five Points, **Garibaldi of Columbia** provides an inviting sophisticated neighborhood atmosphere with an imposing art deco bar, classic Italian offerings, delectable seafood specials, and service with Southern charm and style.

In the Congaree Vista, the **Motor Supply Company** really did supply motor parts throughout Georgia and South Carolina from the 1930s to 1960s. "Motor," known for its excellent wines, artisan cocktails, casual atmosphere and daily-changing, chef-driven menu, works with sustainable, local farms.

Just behind the Stat House, you'll find the **Hunter-Gatherer Brewery** and the traditional English-style ales it brews. You cannot get them anywhere else in the world. Patrons enjoy the fresh, homemade dishes and a low-key atmosphere that attracts interesting, diverse people who come to talk and listen to live music ranging from jazz to alternative and folk.

Ristorante Divino offers Northern Italian cuisine focusing on fresh, local ingredients. Located in the Congaree Vista, it bills itself as Columbia's destination for fine Italian dining. Its superbly trained chefs bring experience and expertise to the table.

Hampton Street Vineyard's extensive wine list is always changing to accommodate wine industry trends. You are in good company here. Some of the artists and wine dignitaries who have dined here include Guy Buffet, Jean Trimbach, Marcel Guigal, Rodney Strong, Tom Murphy, Jeff Kunde, Jed Steel, Eli Parker, and Marcia Mondavi to name a few.

Note: Space restraints mean not all restaurants get mention but that does not mean they aren't wonderful. Visit Columbia Visitors Bureau online and check out its restaurant listings—**www.columbiacvb.com**. As the site says, "Eating in the South is a way of life, and Columbia does it well. From Southern comfort foods to trendy food truck fare, there are many unique dining options throughout the region."

Bon appétit!

fair and unique and funky regional crafts together in a one-day festival. Festival goers see unusual jewelry and crafts that include vintage fabric purses. In its own words, "Sometimes Crafty Feast is indoors and sometimes it is outdoors. Every festival is a little different."

The festival year closes with Columbia's longest running holiday tradition: Riverbanks Zoo & Garden's Lights Before Christmas. Families bring the kids and cameras to see nearly one million twinkling lights. For more than twenty-five years it has been a family tradition.

FAMOUSLY FAMOUS

Great restaurants and celebrities go together, and it is nice to have well-known neighbors. Columbia and the Midlands aren't hurting when it comes to notable residents. Actors, artists, musicians, writers, athletes, astronauts, a Catholic cardinal, and a Nobel Laureate, among others, have called and call Columbia home. Check Columbia's Notable People in Wikipedia and you'll find over 80 famous residents, many of whom are known across the land. Here are but a few.

BLUE SKY, ARTIST. Blue Sky's *Tunnelvision*, a trompe l'oeil painting on the old AgFirst Farm Credit Bank Building appears to pierce the building with a long tunnel as the sun goes down. Sky claims that the idea appeared to him in a dream—a tunnel hewn out of mountain rock. "So the idea for *Tunnelvision* came in a dream," said Sky. "I woke up early in the morning and just sketched it out. I'd already seen the wall. I'd sat and studied it for hours, just waiting to see what would come before my eyes, and nothing came. And early one morning, I woke up and it was there. ...That's where *Tunnelvision* came from." The painting vaulted Blue Sky, née Warren Edward Johnson, to national fame.

CHARLES F. BOLDVEN JR., ASTRONAUT. Retired Marine Corps Major General Charles

THE LIGHTS BEFORE CHRISTMAS BRING A WINTER WONDERLAND TO COLUMBIA; VISITORS FROM FAR AND NEAR COME TO THE ZOO JUST OFF GREYSTONE BOULEVARD NIGHTLY TO SEE THE SPECTACLE DURING THE HOLIDAY SEASON.

Photo by Richard W. Rokes courtesy of Riverbanks Zoo & Garden

Frank Bolden Jr. graduated from C. A. Johnson High School in 1964 and received an appointment to the U.S. Naval Academy. Commissioned as a second lieutenant in the Marine Corps, Bolden completed flight training and became a naval aviator. After his final shuttle flight in 1994, he left NASA and returned to active duty with Marine Corps operating forces as the Deputy Commandant of Midshipmen at the U.S. Naval Academy. The U.S. Astronaut Hall of Fame inducted him as a member in May 2006.

JAMES DICKEY, POET, NOVELIST, & ESSAYIST. A gifted poet but known to many for his powerful novel, *Deliverance*, James Dickey

cut a wide swath not just through Columbia but the country. One of the major mid-century American poets, Dickey is known for his sweeping historical vision and eccentric poetic style. Among his better-known poems

are *The Performance, Cherrylog Road, The Firebombing, May Day Sermon, Falling,* and *For The Last Wolverine.* For many, however, *Deliverance* is the association with this man who was inducted into the fifty-member American Academy of Arts and Letters in 1988.

JAMES DICKEY NEVER WANTED TO BE AN OBSERVER; HE WANTED TO PARTICIPATE. "I'M THE KIND OF PERSON WHO CAN'T BE INTERESTED IN A THING WITHOUT WANTING TO SEE IF I CAN'T GET OUT THERE AND DO A LITTLE OF IT MYSELF. IF I SEE SOMEBODY SHOOTING ARROWS, I WANT TO GET A BOW AND SEE IF I CAN SHOOT SOME MYSELF." THIS SAME THEORY OF WRITING PROPELLED HIS FLIGHT INTO FAME.

BLUE SKY'S *TUNNELVISION* SURPRISES FIRST-TIME OBSERVERS MAKING IT APPEAR AS IF THEY CAN DRIVE INTO A WEST VIRGINIA SUNRISE. CHISELED GRANITE OFFERS THE IMAGINATION A SHORTCUT TO MOUNTAIN VISTAS.

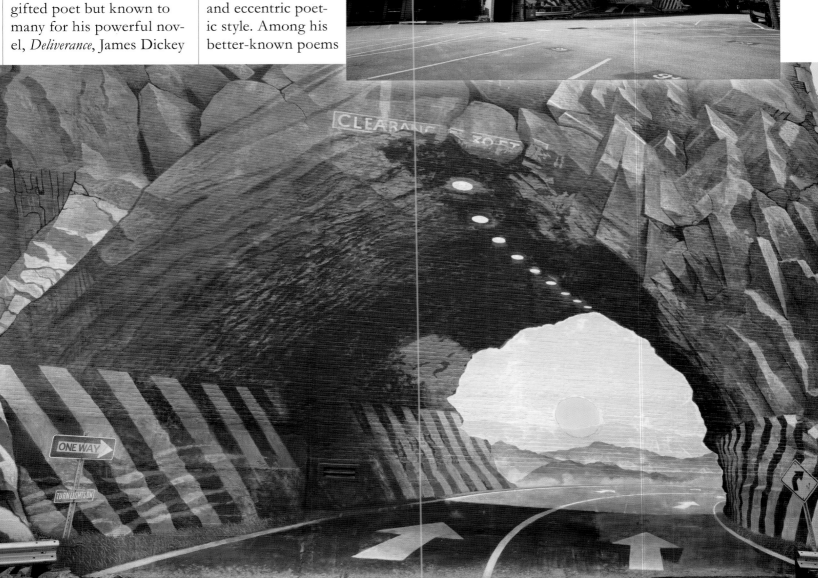

Photos on this page by Paul Ringger

City of rivers, vistas, and dreams

COLUMBIA'S WIKIPEDIA ENTRY LISTS MORE THAN NINETY "NOTABLE PEOPLE" INCLUDING PROFESSIONAL ATHLETES, WRESTLERS, A NOBEL PRIZE WINNER, STEVE SPURRIER (THE OL' BALL COACH), AND ROCK MUSICIANS, AMONG OTHERS. MANY ROSE TO PROMINENCE AS ARTISTS, SONGWRITERS, POETS, AND NOVELISTS. A STRONG CREATIVE SPIRIT LIVES IN COLUMBIA AND PLACES LIKE STUDIO CELLAR, A PUBLIC ART STUDIO, NURTURES FUTURE NOTABLES.

ALEXANDER ENGLISH, FORMER NBA STAR. Alex English, born in Columbia, played for the South Carolina Gamecocks and the National Basketball Association's Denver Nuggets. He averaged 21.5 points and 5.5 rebounds per game during his NBA career and was the NBA's most prolific scorer during the 1980s. Named to eight NBA All-Star teams, the Nuggets retired his No. 2 jersey. He was elected to the Basketball Hall of Fame in 1997.

THE FABULOUS MOOLAH, WWE/WWF FORMER WOMEN'S CHAMPION. The name Lillian Ellison may not ring a bell with sports fans but The Fabulous Moolah will. Her flying drop kicks, flying head scissors and hair-pulling "flying mare" body slams brought her wrestling fame. When it comes to women's wrestling, she stands head and shoulders above the rest. The late Moolah was the longest reigning champion in the history of her sport in a career that spanned over 50 years. Her legacy made her name synonymous with women's wrestling.

DR. KARY MULLIS, SCIENTIST AND NOBEL PRIZE LAUREATE. Kary Mullis received a Nobel Prize in chemistry in 1993 for inventing the polymerase chain reaction. The process, which Mullis conceptualized in 1983, is hailed as one of the monumental scientific techniques of the twentieth century. He graduated from Dreher High School and Georgia Tech and earned a Ph. D. in biochemistry from the University of California, Berkeley. He holds an honorary degree of Doctor of Science from the University of South Carolina.

STEVE SPURRIER, COLLEGE FOOTBALL COACH. Introduced as Carolina's 32nd head coach on November 23, 2004, Steve Spurrier brought a stellar record to Columbia and made Gamecock fans' dreams of fielding winning teams a reality. Spurrier, a national championship coach, has won seven SEC titles, garnered nine conference Coach of the Year awards, and won over 73 percent of the college games he's coached. A two-time All-American quarterback and Heisman Trophy winner for the Florida Gators, he was inducted into the College Football Hall of Fame as a player in 1986. He played professional football for ten seasons during the 1960s and 1970s with the San Francisco 49ers and the Tampa Bay Buccaneers of the National Football League.

THE FABULOUS MOOLAH'S FINAL RESTING PLACE. ▼

Photo © Sephiroth Storm / Wikimedia

DR. KARY MULLIS. ▼

Photo © Dona Mapston / Wikimedia

STEVE SPURRIER. ▼

Photo © Jeff Kern / Wikimedia

Photo © David Shankbone / Wikimedia

ROB THOMAS, LEAD SING-
ER OF MATCHBOX TWENTY.

Rob Thomas grew up in
Lake City, Turbeville, and
Columbia. He became the
youngest-ever member of
the South Carolina Music
and Entertainment Hall of
Fame with good reason. He
has ranked as one of mod-
ern music's more compelling
and commercially successful
artists for more than a decade. In addition to Matchbox Twenty, his solo work
and collaborations with
Santana, Mick Jagger and
Willie Nelson have resulted
in more than 80 million al-
bums sold worldwide.

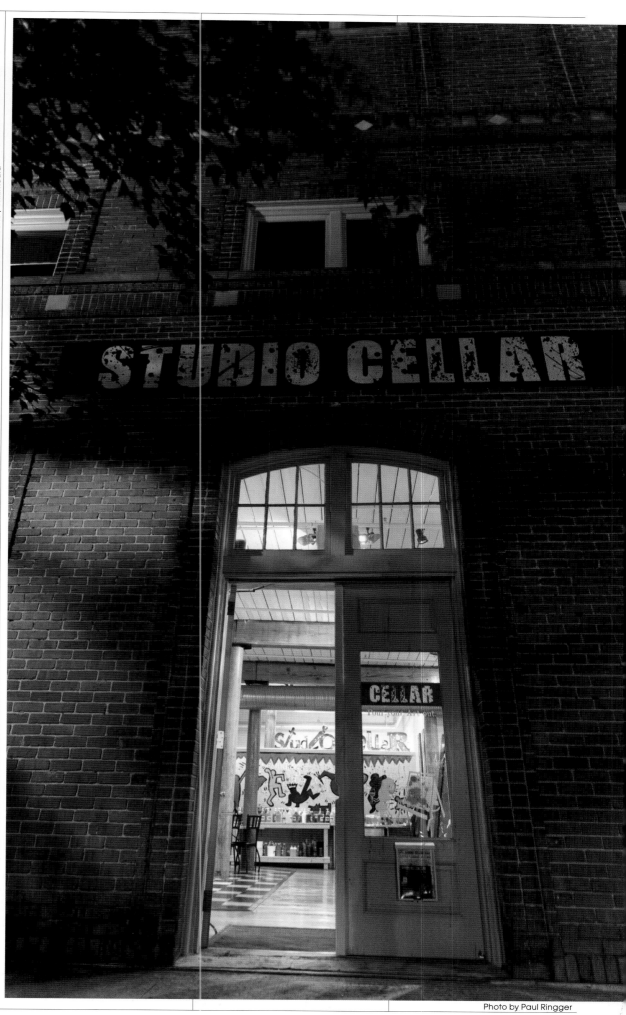

Photo by Paul Ringger

City of rivers, vistas, and dreams

Photo by Paul Ringger

Chapter 5

Center Of Commerce

Columbia and the Midlands are a center of insurance and insurance services, government, and education, and diverse companies and businesses. The climate for commerce is good. According to the Columbia Chamber of Commerce, "The greater Columbia community has made great progress over the past few years to develop a regional vision. This work has led to business growth, improvements in infrastructure, job creation and workforce development, as well as maintaining our status as the most military friendly community in America."

Companies like Orlando-based Nephron Pharmaceuticals Corporation, a global leader in manufacturing generic respiratory medications and contract manufacturing, recently built a 408,000-square-foot state-of-the-art facility in Cayce here in the Midlands. The company will manufacture eye drop medications, anti-cancer drugs, vaccines, and the generic respiratory medicine for which Nephron Pharmaceuticals is known.

Photo by Tom Poland

Online retailer Amazon built a distribution center in West Columbia. In addition to high-tech companies locating in Columbia and the Midlands, the region has a history of developing its own forward-looking companies.

WHERE INSURANCE WENT HIGH TECH

The Midlands has over 100 years of history, innovation, and growth in the insurance technology and services industry. In 1974, G. Larry Wilson began his career with the Seibels Bruce Group, while attending the University of South Carolina. Seeing stacks and stacks of paper, Wilson dreamed of a way to transfer paper-based information to computers—keypunch cards showed him the way to create a Policy Management System (PMS). The software programs Wilson and a seven-member team developed automated premium calculation and billing procedures.

ACADEMIC AND PRIVATE RESEARCH AT INNOVISTA'S HORIZON HAS INCLUDED HYDROGEN FUEL CELLS, ALTERNATIVE ENERGIES, NANOTECHNOLOGY, AND ENVIRONMENTAL SCIENCES. EXPECT BIG THINGS TO COME FROM COLUMBIA IN THESE FIELDS. ▼

As word of this computer-driven business solution spread, other insurance companies asked to buy the system. In 1974, Seibels Bruce created the PMS Division and began selling its programs to the entire property/casualty industry. In 1981, Seibels spun off PMS and it became Policy Management Systems

Corporation, a company that attracted insurance and information technology professionals to Columbia and sowed the seeds for an insurance technology cluster in the Midlands.

By 1994, PMSC had operations in 24 countries and 3,000 software systems licenses in force. The firm's consulting services included the design and management of automation packages for clients.

Today Columbia is hailed as a cluster for insurance companies and software and services providers to the insurance industry. Companies such as Colonial Life, Blue-Cross BlueShield of South Carolina, and lean-but-agile high-tech insurance systems

and services providers cement that legacy.

The Columbia Insurance Technology Services Cluster (iTs|SC) is a New Carolina cluster promoting Greater Columbia's wealth of opportunities within the insurance technology sector. iTs|SC's vision is to grow the industry's employers, which now employ nearly 15,000 in the region, into the world's largest, most dynamic, and most competitive insurance technology cluster.

FOREVER FUEL—HYDROGEN FUEL CELL LEADERSHIP

Clearly, hydrogen fuel cells could revolutionize the way the world makes and uses energy, and Columbia is doing its part to make it happen. The

Photos on this page by Paul Ringger

USC–Columbia Fuel Cell Collaborative, formed by the University of South Carolina, the City of Columbia, EngenuitySC, and SCRA, hope to position Columbia as a leader in hydrogen fuel cell innovation and technology. The mission is to attract private sector partners, top fuel cell scientists, entrepreneurs, and innovators to the region to grow a fuel cell technology innovation pipeline from discovery to development and deployment.

INNOVISTA

Innovista, the University of South Carolina's economic development arm, connects businesses, industry, and entrepreneurs with university resources. So doing helps create jobs, accelerate innovation, and drive economic prosperity not just in the Midlands and South Carolina but around the world. The 500-acre district in the heart of Columbia brings state government and educational and cultural elements together. Innovista—USC's dream for reinventing the notion of how and where researchers live and work—brings innovation, creativity, entertainment, culture, and more to the Midlands.

THE PEACE KEEPERS—WHERE DREAMS OF PEACE BECOME REALITY

Fort Jackson. I-77 skirts Columbia's eastern edge. This stretch of interstate midway between New York City and Miami sends hurried travelers through Columbia and the Midlands. Many may not realize they are passing this bastion of defense, Fort Jackson. Having shaped the history of the United States, indeed, the world, for close to 100 years, the Fort continues to influence the economy and character of Columbia and the Midlands. Fort Jackson remains the only army base in the United States within a city, and for Columbia and its neighbors this is a prosperous, good thing.

SOLDIERS AND RESERVISTS RECEIVE BASIC COMBAT TRAINING AT FORT JACKSON. THE PROGRAM TAKES TEN WEEKS TO COMPLETE. EACH YEAR, THE FORT GRADUATES 36,000 BCT PERSONNEL.

NOT ALL WORK: SOLDIERS, FAMILY MEMBERS AND CIVILIANS ENJOY A 'BIG DAY OUT' AT SEMMES LAKE, INCLUDING A REGATTA FEATURING BOATS MADE OF RECYCLED MATERIALS (BELOW). RUNNERS PARTICIPATE IN FORT JACKSON'S ANNUAL RUN FOR THE FALLEN (BOTTOM).

Photos (above) © Susanne Kappler, Fort Jackson Leader / Wikimedia

The famous and the unknown, the driven and drifters, have bonded at Fort Jackson with singular vision: preserving freedom. Fort Jackson trains soldiers in basic combat training, and it is a breeding ground for history. Its story began in 1916. A cold January rain fell as military and civilian planners climbed a sand knoll overlooking pineland six miles east of Columbia. They dreamed of establishing a new defense facility. The planners' mission was crucial to the War Department: evaluating a site for a US Army training center. The site was good, and the Columbia Chamber of Commerce raised $59,000 to turn the Colonel Wade Hampton's Estate over to the government.

Consider but a few of Fort Jackson's historic highlights. The headquarters' flagpole, which stood at the 1938 World's Fair in New York City, was a gift from New York Mayor Fiorello LaGuardia.

Sandy Spring's Corporal Freddie Stowers, the grandson of a slave and the only black Medal of Honor recipient from World War I, trained here.

One hot night, Lieutenants Briton Hadden and Henry Luce walked back to their barrack discussing "a paper" they would found. TIME magazine resulted.

The soldiers marching in unison and learning warfare make history, and celebrities and world leaders have rightfully come to pay them homage. Betty Grable, *Life* cover girl, came. Bob Hope came. On June 24, 1942, Winston Churchill stepped from a train at Fort Jackson. Watching thousands of recruits training, Churchill said, "They're just like money in the bank." General Jimmy Doolittle came to Fort Jackson in 1992 and 1993. President Roosevelt twice visited the fort.

When Midlands' residents see soldiers in pressed khakis, they think peace and prosperity and thank them for their service to the country. They are here because of a dream that began close to 100 years ago.

McEntire Air Base. The South Carolina Air National Guard's (SCANG) 169th Fighter Wing flies the F-16 Fighting Falcon, a single-seat, multi-purpose fighter that can fly at Mach two while performing air-to-air and air-to-ground tactical missions. McEntire Air Base, previously known as Congaree Air Base, served as a World War II U.S. Marine Corps training base. It, too, has a proud history.

SCANG has been called to active military service for numerous historic contingencies. SCANG Airmen served during the Korean War at various installations in the United States and abroad. In late 1961, SCANG served during the Berlin Crisis. In late 1990, activated

OUTDOOR EXHIBITS ON DISPLAY AT THE U.S. ARMY BASIC COMBAT TRAINING MUSEUM AT FORT JACKSON INCLUDE A HELICOPTER AND BATTLE TANKS. ▼

Photo © Andrew McIntyr / Wikimedia

units of the SCANG deployed to Saudi Arabia for Operation Desert Shield/Storm, flying 2,000 combat missions and dropping four million pounds of munitions, while maintaining the highest aircraft mission capable rate in the theater. The unit flew to Baghdad and took out surface-to-air missiles without casualties. Weeks later, the men from McEntire returned to their home base with the exact force that left: over 700 people, 40 pilots, and 24 F-16s.

Thanks to Fort Jackson and McEntire Air Base, Columbia and the Midlands possess a proud military heritage, one that has played a key role in peace around the word and prosperity at home.

A Tire Manufacturer

In the early 1980s Michelin opened a new plant in Lexington, South Carolina. Michelin set the stage for giving South Carolina a chance to lead the country in tire manufacturing. Today with Bridgestone, Michelin, Continental, and Giti all manufacturing tires in South Carolina, the state has become the country's number one producer of tires and the Midlands plays a big role in that distinction.

F-16 FIGHTING FALCON AIRCRAFT FROM THE 157TH FIGHTER SQUADRON, SOUTH CAROLINA AIR NATIONAL GUARD PREPARE FOR TAKEOFF DURING AN OPERATIONAL READINESS EVALUATION AT McENTIRE JOINT NATIONAL GUARD BASE. ▼

Photo ©vv Master Sgt. Marvin R. Preston / Wikimedia

F-16 FIGHTING FALCON AIRCRAFT FROM THE 169TH FIGHTER WING SIT IN A HANGAR BAY ON McENTIRE JOINT NATIONAL GUARD BASE DURING AN EVALUATION OF THE UNIT'S ABILITY TO LAUNCH MISSIONS WHILE IN A CHEMICAL WARFARE ENVIRONMENT. ▼ ▼

U.S. AIR FORCE LT. COL. TERRENCE HEDLEY, A FIGHTER PILOT WITH THE 157TH FIGHTER SQUADRON OUT OF McENTIRE JOINT NATIONAL GUARD BASE, S.C., PREPARES TO TAKE OFF FROM JOINT BASE BALAD, IRAQ. ▼

Photo © Tech. Sgt. Caycee Cook / Wikimedia

Photo © SMSgt Edward E. Snyder / Wikimedia

Chapter 6

A Cool Way Of Life Is Hot

A CITY OF MUSEUMS

Columbia's diverse museums range from art to military to law enforcement and more. The South Carolina State Museum, the state's largest, most comprehensive museum, sits along the banks of the Congaree River in downtown Columbia. Founded in 1988, it tells the history of South Carolina through rich and diverse collections displayed through interactive and engaging exhibitions. The museum's four floors of permanent exhibits cover history, art, natural history and science and technology. Visitors see displays on   dinosaurs, pre-historic fossils, the Revolutionary War, Civil War, African-American history, and more. Children and adults alike love 'Finn,' the museum's giant pre-historic megalodon shark replica.

Four disciplines reflect South Carolina's rich history: South Carolina art, natural history, science and technology, and cultural history, all backed by more than 70,000 artifacts.

Summer 2104 saw the museum open a one-of-a-kind facility—the only observatory of its kind in the nation, one of the Southeast's largest planetariums, and South Carolina's only permanent 4D

Photo by Jay Browne

City of rivers, vistas, and dreams

Photo by John Nelson

McKISSICK MUSEUM EXAMINES THE DIVERSITY OF THE CULTURE AND GE-
OGRAPHY OF THE SOUTH WITH EXHIBITIONS LIKE *TRADITIONS, CHANGE, AND
CELEBRATION: NATIVE ARTISTS OF THE SOUTHEAST*, AUGUST 8, 2014 - JULY
25, 2015.

theater. Nowhere else in the country will you find all three innovative elements and a multidisciplinary museum focusing on art, history, natural history, and science/technology under one roof. The 75,000-square-foot renovation and expansion project, "Windows to New Worlds," puts the State Museum on education's cutting edge, particularly in science, technology, engineering, and mathematics.

Founded in 1950, the Columbia Museum of Art opened its new building on Main Street in 1998, transforming an urban department store into a sleek and airy, light-filled space with 25 galleries. Its collections, exhibitions, and programs engage the mind and enrich the spirit. You'll find a world-class collection of European and American fine and decorative art that spans centuries here. Collections include masterpieces of the Italian Renaissance and Baroque from the Samuel H. Kress Collection, works by significant furniture and silver makers, and modern and contemporary art from the present time. The museum also offers changing exhibitions from renowned museums and educational programs that include group and public tours, lectures, films and concert series.

Other museums include the University of South Carolina's McKissick Museum, which tells the story of Southern life, the South Carolina Confederate Relic

Photo courtesy of Columbia Art Museum

ART AND EDUCATION ARE PARTNERS AT THE COLUMBIA MUSEUM OF ART. WHILE IT DOESN'T LEND BOOKS, THE MUSEUM'S LORICK LIBRARY LETS RESEARCH-
ERS ACCESS ITS INFORMATION. EXHIBITIONS, SPECIAL EVENTS, AND RESEARCH ATTRACT OVER 6,000 VISITORS A MONTH TO THE MUSEUM AND ITS MORE THAN
20,000 SQUARE FEET OF GALLERY SPACE.

Room and Military Museum, the Cayce Historical Museum, and Lexington County Museum.

The Seat Of Power

In 1788, following the relocation of the capital from Chvvarleston to Columbia, work began on the State House, designed by James Hoban of Charleston. The legislature first met in this State House in 1790 and it impressed President Washington when he visited Columbia in 1791. By the 1840's, however, the State House had deteriorated and required frequent repairs.

General William T. Sherman and his Union army captured the State House on February 17, 1865. Burned, rebuilt, and remodeled over the years, the State House is the centerpiece of South Carolina's government. Beset by construction problems, war, and the need for renovation, the grand old building nonetheless stands as an imposing edifice with beautiful grounds featuring monuments and statuary. Built of blue granite from a nearby quarry, it took 56 years to complete the capital. From far and near, people come to see the grounds and see this place of grand visions with its copper Greek Revival dome and Corinthian columns. They come, too, to see those six bronze stars that mark where Union cannonballs struck the building.

A Renowned Zoo & Botanical Garden

In the early 1960s, a group of local businessmen initiated the concept of a small community zoo. Known as the Columbia Zoo, the proposed facility was designed exclusively as a children's zoo with a nursery rhyme theme. Following legislation and collaboration between Richland and Lexington Counties, the dream became a reality. Riverbanks opened April 25, 1974. Today over 2,000 animals enthrall, amuse, and outright surprise visitors. Between the zoo's wildlife and the botanical garden's flora, a day here is like a trip around the world.

Horticulture magazine praised the botanical garden as "one of 10 gardens that inspire." HGTV calls it "one of 20 great public gardens across America." Something is always blooming at the garden. The gardens are themed, too. There's the Collection Garden where 100 different milk and wine lilies grow. There's the Old Rose Garden where you'll find the world's largest collection of noisettes. Kids love the Play Garden, which features a playhouse and secret play garden. If seventy acres of botanical beauty don't bring out the gardener in you, nothing will.

At the West Columbia entrance you'll see the Bog Garden with its large waterfall. See, too, the carnivorous pitcher plants and water lilies. The large boulders will give you a sense of being in the mountains, and be sure to walk the nature trail whose highlights include the old Saluda Mill ruins and its lonesome but winsome keystone arch, testaments to Sherman's march through Columbia.

Theatres

There's no shortage of theatres in the Midlands. Columbians and regional thespian enthusiasts have a variety of stage presentations to enjoy year-round.

Founded in 1988 by famed puppeteer Allie Scollon and son John, the **Columbia**

Long associated with the zoo, Caribbean flamingoes bring a tropical splash of pink that pleases crowds, especially children. In March 2014, the last remaining member of the zoo's original animal collection died. It was a Caribbean flamingo, a charter member, that joined the zoo in September 1973. ▼

Photo by Paul Ringger

City of rivers, vistas, and dreams

Marionette Theatre entertains and educates children and adults through the artistry of puppetry. Originally housed in a turn-of-the-century Vista warehouse, the theatre moved in 1995 to its

Photo courtesy of the Columbia Marionette Theatre

SOMETIMES FUN COMES WITH STRINGS ATTACHED, ESPECIALLY IF YOU ATTEND THE COLUMBIA MARIONETTE THEATER WHERE THIS ANCIENT FORM OF ENTERTAINMENT TAKES PLACE. PEOPLE OFTEN REFER TO THE PUPPET'S CONTROLLER AS A "PUPPETEER." THE FORMAL TERM IS "MASTERMINDER." EVIDENCE INDICATES MASTERMINDERS PUT ON PUPPET SHOWS AS LONG AGO AS 2000 BC IN EGYPT.

current location near Riverfront Park. It was rededicated as The Allie Scollon Puppetry Center in 2006.

Founded by Gene and Catherine Eaker and their daughter, Genie, **The Patchwork Players** is a nationally known professional touring theater and is Columbia's longest-running children's theater.

Trustus Theatre is an award-winning professional non-profit theatre. Located in the Congaree Vista, Trustus presents thought-provoking entertainment in a comfortable, unique setting. Trustus consists of two theatres, the 134-seat Thigpen Mainstage Theatre and the 50-seat intimate Richard and Debbie Cohn Side Door Theatre.

Workshop Theatre has long been the creative domain of many of the area's most talented actors, directors, and technicians. **Columbia Children's Theatre** is the Midlands' premiere theatre for families and young audiences. **Harbison Theatre**, a 400-seat state-of-the-art facility, stages music, theatre, dance, comedy, and more. Other theatres include Lexington's **Village Square Theatre**, **On State Productions**, and the **South Carolina Shakespeare Company**.

USC's Department of Theatre and Dance production program, **Theatre South Carolina**, extends classroom teaching into its live productions. **Town Theater** enjoys the largest regular audience with close to 30,000 patrons of all ages. Many of its performers have appeared on Broadway, network television, and in major feature films such as *Cats*, *A Chorus Line*, *Ruthless People*, *Hill Street Blues*, and *North and South*. **Stage 5** brings live theatre to Columbia and the surrounding area. Its mission is to bring quality theatrical events, choral presentations, musical productions, and productions from new writers, directors, and actors into the medium of theatre.

In Columbia and the Midlands, curtains are always on the rise.

A WATERY PARADISE

Beautiful homes and boats aplenty—that's Lake Murray. Besides being a haven for wildlife, it is a sought-after place by man as well. *Boating* magazine named it one the top ten places to live and boat. Its 650 miles of shoreline wash over four counties bringing beauty to the Midlands. From casual anglers to pros, its striper and bass lure many. Summer weekends find boaters rafting up to enjoy the "Lake Murray lifestyle." Close to sundown when the water is like glass, skiers etch feathery traces onto its coves.

Whether a bungalow, gated community, or palatial mansion, homes on Lake Murray are coveted possessions, and the lake even has a magazine devoted to its coverage, *Lake Murray Magazine*. There's much to cover from regattas to wakeboarding, tubing, skiing, and palatial homes.

Marinas, campgrounds, landings and boat ramps, and Dreher Island State Park, spanning three islands, and 348 acres, gives people access to twelve miles of Lake Murray shoreline.

While the water itself is a beautiful vista, forests and sweeps of land where old farmsteads run up against new homes speak to the way dreams and visions transform rural areas into a watery playground.

Restaurants such as the Rusty Anchor and Liberty Tap Room, the Frayed Knot Bar & Grill, and Spinner's Resort & Marina please boaters and land-bound patrons.

Lake Murray, a setting with its share of romance, is a place for love. A famous tourist spot in Paris, the Pont des Arts footbridge, is known for its love locks, a permanent way to eternalize and symbolize unbreakable love for another. Paris's "love locks" have crossed the Atlantic to festoon the fence at Lake Murray's dam

Photo by Stephanie Norwood

and what a view from here. On one side an expanse of water flecked white with sailboats; on the other side, a distant view of the "Famously Hot" Columbia.

SEC Football

As a member of the dominant Southeastern Conference, the University of South Carolina Gamecocks enjoy high visibility nationwide. It is no shock that all roads lead to Williams-Bryce Stadium come autumn. With flags fluttering on SUVs, trucks, and motor homes, the Gamecock nation faithfully come to watch their team take on all comers in football.

Click here for love. Many starry-eyed couples stop on the Dreher Shoals dam walking path to honor the European custom of locking their love above the water, a quirky art installation symbolising unbreakable love. ◄

Lake Murray is more than a recreational lake. It's a liquid interstate for the many families who inhabit its shores or visit via watercraft. Forty-one miles long and fourteen miles across at its widest point, its 48,000 surface acres provide an infinite number of routes from here to there. ▼

Photo by Stephanie Norwood

City of rivers, vistas, and dreams

THE WORKS PROGRESS ADMINISTRATION BUILT WHAT WAS CAROLINA STADIUM IN 1934. AT THAT TIME IT SEATED 17,600. THE STADIUM CONSISTENTLY RANKS AMONG THE TOP 20 IN ATTENDANCE. ▶

THE KOGER CENTER, "COLUMBIA'S HOME FOR THE PERFORMING ARTS," HOSTS BALLET, PHILHARMONIC PERFORMANCES, SPEAKERS, AND THE ANNUAL NUTCRACKER, PRESENTED BY THE COLUMBIA CITY BALLET. ▶▼

BUILT IN 2004, THE COLUMBIA METROPOLITAN CONVENTION CENTER PROVIDES A FLEXIBLE, BEAUTIFUL MEETING SPACE THAT HOSTS INTIMATE MEETINGS AND LARGE GALAS. TEN FINE HOTELS WITHIN A MILE OF THE CENTER, MOST WITHIN .7 OF A MILE, MAKE IT HIGHLY CONVENIENT TO OUT-OF-TOWN EXHIBITORS AND VISITORS. ▼

Competing in the Football Bowl Subdivision of the National Collegiate Athletics Association and the Southeastern Conference's Eastern Division has been the most successful since Steve Spurrier assumed head coaching duties. Williams-Brice Stadium and its 80,250 fans are witnessing the golden era of Gamecock football.

VENUES

Residents of Columbia, the Midlands, and visitors outside the region and state come to Columbia to see the world's top performers and artists, as visionary leaders have given the area excellent venues. The Colonial Life Arena, the largest arena in the state of South Carolina with 18,000 seats and the tenth largest on-campus basketball facility in the nation, sits on the University of South Carolina campus. A one-of-a-kind facility,

it features 41 suites, four entertainment suites, and the Frank McGuire Club, a full-service hospitality room with a capacity of 300. The University of South Carolina's Athletic Department is the primary owner and operator of the Colonial Life Arena, ranked 22nd in the world for total tickets sold in 2003 by *Pollstar Magazine.*

The Columbia Metropolitan Convention Center, a 142,500-square-foot facility, with a 24,700-square-foot, column-free exhibit hall and a 17,135-square-foot ballroom hosts events such as the SC Book Festival where high-profile writers including Pat Conroy draw huge crowds.

Williams-Brice Stadium, capacity 80,250, home to the USC Gamecocks is one of the finest facilities in college football. Carolina annually

ranks among the nation's leaders in attendance and Gamecock fans, regarded as some of the country's most loyal, even during winless seasons dream of championships. The stadium's The Zone features an 11,000-square foot banquet facility and provides fans a panoramic view from the South End Zone.

The Koger Center for the Arts, USC's and Columbia's performing arts center, can seat over 2,400 guests and produces a performing arts series each year titled "Koger Presents."

Carolina Stadium, on the banks of the Congaree River, provides a beautiful setting for the University of South Carolina Gamecocks baseball team and its legacy of repeat champions in the College World Series. The largest baseball stadium in

Photo by Paul Ringger

South Carolina, it was built at a cost of $35.6 million.

Township Auditorium seats 3,200. The Columbia architectural firm of Lafaye and Lafaye designed and constructed the Georgian Revival building in 1930. The Township has hosted thousands of events from concerts to conventions to wrestling matches. Listed in the National Register of Historic Places it received a $12

Photos this page by Jay Browne

MIDLAND'S WILDLIFE SCULPTOR GRAINGER MCKOY CLIMBED UPHILL IN AN ART WORLD THAT REFUSED TO RECOGNIZE WOOD AS A CLASSICAL ART MEDIUM. HE PERSISTED, EVER CHALLENGING HIMSELF. IN 1974 HIS FIRST EXHIBIT TOOK PLACE AT NEW YORK'S AMERICAN MUSEUM OF ART. HE CONTINUES TO EXHIBIT IN PRESTIGIOUS MUSEUMS.

BLACK SWANS TAKE THEIR PLACE AMONG THE SWANS AT SWAN LAKE IRIS GARDEN. THEY TYPICALLY BREED IN THE SOUTHEAST AND SOUTHWEST REGIONS OF AUSTRALIA. YOU'LL SEE THEM "DOWN UNDER" AT THE GARDENS WHEN THEY TIP OVER TO FEED ON AQUATIC PLANTS.

A PEACH ORCHARD EXPLODING IN PINK BLOSSOMS RANKS AMONG THE MORE BEAUTIFUL SCENES IN THE MIDLANDS. TRUCKS LOADED WITH BASKETS OF PEACHES ON BACK ROADS ARE A FAMILIAR SIGHT. DESTINATION? PIES, ICE CREAM, AND PRESERVES.

million interior and exterior renovation.

Charlie W. Johnson Stadium is the home field for Benedict College's football and soccer teams. The $12 million state-of-the-art stadium has a seating capacity of 10,000, which can be expanded to 15,000. Located on 61-acres, the stadium features modernized accommodations on three levels.

A SHORT DRIVE AWAY

Columbia sits in a perfect place for exploring South Carolina. Part of a city's allure is its "getaway" factor, and the eight-county Midlands sparkles with day trip venues. Columbia, being centrally located, makes for a great base camp. Choose any point of the compass you like, and an exciting adventure is just a short drive away.

Swan Lake Iris Gardens. The accidental garden in Sumter, referred to by *Southern Living* as a "lovely mistake," developed into one of the finest botanical gardens in the United States. It came about as an accident sure enough. In 1927, Hamilton Carr Bland, a local businessman, was developing 30 acres of swamp and landscaping his home with Japanese iris. But the iris just wouldn't cooperate. After consulting horticulturists, Bland told his gardener to dig up the bulbs and throw them in the swamp. The next spring, the iris exploded into bloom. This "lovely mistake" developed into one of the country's finest botanical gardens.

You will see a lot of wildlife here. Black water studded by cypress knees hosts various waterfowl. The only public park in the United States to feature all eight swan species, Swan Lake Iris

Gardens is also home to some of the nation's most intensive plantings of Japanese iris, which bloom yearly in mid to late May and last until the beginning of June. The garden also boasts many other floral attractions, including colorful camellias, azaleas, day lilies, and Japanese magnolias. A Braille Trail enables the sight-impaired to enjoy the

Photos on pages 78-79 by Paul Ringger

scents and sensations of the gardens.

Here, too, you will find a butterfly garden and a striking sculpture, Grainger McKoy's *Recovery Wing.* His dramatic eighteen-foot sculpture of stainless steel represents the wing of a pintail duck in flight. According to McKoy, "This wing position is considered the weakest in bird flight, yet in

know they still taste like vegetables. The Chocolate Garden also grows flowers with chocolate-colored leaves, or stems, or centers of flowers, as well as chocolate-looking grasses and a chocolate Mimosa tree.

More than 250,000 people visit the Swan Lake Iris Gardens each year. Many come from afar, possibly having seen it featured in

would delight the legendary artist. That little highway will take you through Ridge Spring, Ward, and Johnston towards Edgefield where you'll find expanses of pink peach orchards blooming and things other than peaches—all that start with a "P."

When a carpet of pink cloaks the sandy hills, you'll see a sight that has seduced

the artist's eye is the position with the most beauty and grace. All of us are in recovery somewhere in our lives, as is our environment, of which Swan Lake is a unique part."

A curiosity is the Chocolate Garden, a whimsical addition. Now, warn the kids that these plants are not really chocolate. No sampling allowed! Edible plants such as chocolate cherry tomatoes, chocolate corn, and chocolate mini bell peppers all have a chocolate look but, alas, the kids will be sad to

Southern Living and *Better Homes & Gardens.* It may be viewed "up close and personal" via walking trails and boardwalks.

Peach Country. Drive west from Columbia through Lexington County and you will find a place Vincent Van Gogh would have loved— South Carolina Peach Country. Van Gogh found a sense of renewal in the peach tree's delicate blossoms and so will you. Feeling plucky? Make your way to Highway 23, which threads through acres of peach trees that surely

many a photographer. Watch the farm reports so you can catch the orchards in full bloom and later make a return trip to get split-oak baskets filled with sweet Carolina sunshine: a treat hard to resist. (The split oak baskets will come in handy.) In 1984, the peach became South Carolina's official fruit with good reason. A tree-ripened peach may well be the greatest-tasting

Pearl Harbor fanned the flames of anti-Japanese sentiment and Wells Japanese Garden had to close during World War II because of fears of vandalism. Today, all is peaceful in this garden that's on the National Register of Historic Places. ▶

Besides historic buildings, you'll see unusual art in Edgefield: randomly placed turkey statues sporting wild colors only artists could dream up. One turkey's tail feathers fan out like red, white, and blue bunting. Edgefield is home to the National Wild Turkey Federation. ▶

In Spann Church's cemetery a statue of Clinton Ward stands atop his grave and stares at a distant water tank with the town name, "Ward," painted on it. Nearby a stag tops the resting place of another Ward forbearer, W.H. Ryder. ▼ ▼

fruit of all. Loving care attends this state fruit. When peaches turn a creamy yellow, they are tender and easily bruised, so hands pluck peaches, not machines. Drive through peach country and soon you will see "Peaches For Sale" signs where trucks loaded with baskets of peaches back up to the road.

Your journey will take you through Ward where you will spot an exceptional cemetery beside Spann Methodist Church. The church had its start around 1805 as part of the plantation of John Spann Jr. The cemetery came to be in 1840. Ward's founder, Clinton Ward, wife Martha, and only child, Josephine, sleep here. Josephine stands atop her monument. She died at six. Ward, with his period-vogue lamb chops, stands atop a tall monument but Martha merely has a large sphere atop hers. See the cast iron statue of a deer at the cemetery gate. The statue of a dog by a tree stands near the railroad track. Ward's marker, his wife's, the deer, and the dog made

the Smithsonian's Inventory of American Sculpture. The church and its cemetery made the National Register of Historic Places. Not your ordinary graveyard.

Travel on to Edgefield, the home of ten governors, and you will spot artsy turkeys at street corners. (Edgefield is home to the National Wild Turkey Federation.) The ten governors are Andrew Pickens, George McDuffie, Pierce Mason Butler, James H. Hammond, Francis W. Pickens, Milledge Luke Bonham, John C. Sheppard, Benjamin R. Tillman, John Gary Evans, and J. Strom Thurmond.

Photo © Bill Fitzpatrick / Wikimedia

Edgefield has a history of potters, too. Plantations led to a demand for large-scale food storage and preservation. In the 1800s, slaves made alkaline glazed, traditional pottery as they had in Africa. Notable were the "grotesques" or "voodoo jugs" upon which slave potters applied facial features.

Peaches, politicians, and pottery—that's what a day trip to Peach Country delivers.

The Land of the Rising Sun. North, straight up from Columbia on I-26, you will discover Wells Japanese Garden. Bliss, beauty, and botanical gems featuring a touch of Asia are closer than you think. An easy 42-mile drive to Newberry transports you to the Land of the Rising Sun where Wells Japanese Garden, a Newberry landmark, brings a delightful touch of the Orient to the Midlands. The gardens are on Lindsay Street behind City Hall.

Spring is a great time to walk its trails and enjoy water features and exotic flora. The Japanese perfected the

Photo by Tom Poland

Photo © Bill Fitzpatrick / Wikimedia

art of relaxing and you can thank W. Fulmer Wells, an architecture graduate, for designing Newberry's Japanese garden in 1930. The young Newberry resident studied architecture in California where he visited a Japanese Tea Garden at San Francisco's Golden Gate Park. Legend has it Newberry's garden took root there. His father, W. Fulmer Wells Sr., built the garden. We can rightfully describe this garden as a Japanese-American garden. While its design is Japanese, it was built using local

Photo © Bill Fitzpatrick / Wikimedia

THE NEWBERRY OPERA HOUSE HAS BEEN DESCRIBED AS "FRENCH GOTHIC-INSPIRED." ITS ORIGINAL DESIGN DESIGNATED A FIRST FLOOR SPACE AS A FIRE ENGINE ROOM, COUNCIL CHAMBERS, CLERK'S OFFICE, POLICE OFFICES, AND THREE JAIL CELLS. IT COST $30,000 TO BUILD IN 1881 BUT 1996 RENOVATIONS AND ADDITIONS COST $5,500,000 MAKING IT A STATE-OF-THE-ART PERFORMANCE VENUE.

Photo © Bill Fitzpatrick / Wikimedia

materials. The Wells family donated the garden to the city of Newberry in 1970. Today it is a city park, but not just any park. It is a place of serenity and reflection.

Peace and beauty are yours when you enter the garden through a Torii Gate, a traditional Japanese style gate often found at temple entrances. Torii translates to "where birds reside." Torii, traditionally, are painted red. You'll find other charming Japanese architectural elements: a temple, moon bridge, and teahouse, all of which frame and overlook two small ponds. The posts of the Tea House, incidentally, originally supported the balcony at the Newberry Opera House. The moon bridge spans a small creek that flows through this unique garden. It is tranquil.

Anyone who loves gardens and gardening will appreciate the Egyptian lotus, Japanese iris, water lilies, crepe myrtles, dogwood, and cypress. Concrete bridges, executed in a Japanese design, span the ponds. Of particular interest are cinnamon ferns that flaunt "cinnamon sticks." Large clumps of cinnamon ferns grow in the park's damp woods and creek banks. Note the clusters of sori, which make spores, source of new ferns. But this is just one such plant you can see at this surprising Oriental oasis maintained by the Newberry Council of Garden Clubs.

You will find Wells Japanese Garden in Newberry among other attractions that include the Newberry

Opera House, antique shops, nearby Carter & Holmes Orchids, and a range of restaurants sure to please your and your fellow travelers' taste. The architectural centerpiece of Newberry is the opera house, which came to be in 1881. A mere $30,000 built this Victorian civic eclectic opera house. Three local brickyards and a nearby granite quarry provided construction materials. Known as the entertainment center of the Midlands early on, it hosted a great variety of entertainment: New York plays, minstrels, lecturers, magicians, singers, and boxers. Public protest saved the house from destruction in 1959.

A Place Called Prosperity. It is close by, just 36 miles, and it brings to mind Sheriff Andy's Mayberry. Columned, Southern homes stand at the edge of town and live oaks shade lawns sequestered within white picket fences. Driving through its outskirts you get the feeling Prosperity is a peaceful, happy place. "Prosperity." The name even sounds right. Kind of like the title of a Norman Rockwell painting.

Chartered in 1851 as "Frog Level," such a name deserves an explanation. One legend claims an old man had one too many draws on the bottle and fell asleep by a pond. When he awoke, he thought the croaking frogs were crying "frog level." In 1873, at the insistence of most residents, the Legislature changed the name to "Prosperity."

There is a timeless quality here, the feeling you get around stones, old trees, and buildings from another era. Consider the Prosperity Drug Company on North Main Street. Open since 1895, its marble fountain counter is the real deal. No faux marble here. Along the front and beneath it, are thirteen panels of beautiful marble, their origin a mystery.

Prosperity is not hurting for international fare. Wendy Steiner's Gasthouse zur Elli has operated since 1999. She grew up in Bavaria in a town smaller than Prosperity. "In Germany," she said, "when you live in a big town, you always drive out of town into the country to a restaurant and have a good time there. When you are in a German restaurant, there is no fast food. You go in, you drink, you enjoy yourself with all the other people, then you eat, and then you drink again, and that's your weekend. That's the way it is in Germany."

In the past, folks in Prosperity have used "Main Street to Lake Murray" as a sort of tagline, a rallying cry for local businesses. Sure enough, Main Street leads right to Lake Murray. These days the motto is "Prosperity, SC ... Equal To The Name."

If you want to see gorgeous furniture with a past and a future, peer through the windows of Lowell Dowd and his father, Edwin's, Dixie Heartpine Inc. If the front of their building on North Main reminds you

of a weathered old Southern smokehouse, well it should. Blackened weatherboard fronts it. Harvested in the 1880s, the wood was anywhere from 200 to 800 years old at harvest time. "That wood was here before Christopher Columbus discovered America," said Lowell. "Some of it is 1,000 years old."

The Dowds scour the countryside seeking old buildings concealing longleaf pine beneath old paint and weathering. Longleaf pine was the tree of choice for America's first settlers, but today less than 10,000 grow wild. The Dowds carefully salvage the wood and custom-build heartpine furniture. Lowell ran his hand over a beautiful table pointing out the original nail holes. "We don't stress the wood," he said. "Over 125 years stresses it enough."

The natural, red patina of Heartpine (also called 'heartwood') bestows a radiant glow to the Dowds' store and walking amid the beautiful pieces is very much like walking back in time. Hand-hewn beams, mantels, antique chairs? They are here and so are some interesting murals. Check out the rehabilitated train depot too, all less than an hour away in neighboring Newberry County.

Chapter 7

A Place Of Higher Learning

Institutions of higher learning enrich Columbia and the Midlands. No matter where you go in the Midlands, you will see beautiful campuses where people of many talents and inclinations are preparing for the future. The Midlands, in fact, has a long and proud history of providing outstanding educations to a diverse populace. Backed by a strong community of teachers, professors, administrators, and educational associations, higher learning thrives in the South Carolina Midlands, and innovative public and private schools prepare students for the challenges of tomorrow.

The South Carolina State Board for Technical and Comprehensive Education, based in Columbia, oversees the state's technical college system, a network of sixteen technical colleges, a system of education that has long attracted some of the world's most innovative companies to South Carolina. It's no accident that companies like Michelin, Amazon, and Nephron Pharmaceuticals established bases in the Midlands. As early as the early 1960s, state leaders developed a strategy for attracting top-flight companies and thereby transforming South Carolina's destiny. To stop an exodus of workers from the state, state leaders

Photo by Paul Ringger

City of rivers, vistas, and dreams

ALLEN UNIVERSITY GREW FROM THE AFRICAN METHODIST EPISCOPAL CHURCH'S DESIRE TO EDUCATE FREED SLAVES AND TO ENSURE THAT THE CHURCH HAD READY ACCESS TO AN EDUCATED CLERGY.

Photos on pages 86-87 by Paul Ringger

developed a new system to educate people for the practicalities of careers in manufacturing. Midlands Technical College, part of that system, operates seven campuses that provide the very latest training and education that prepares students for a future where technology will be increasingly important.

Thanks to the state's technical training program and other institutions of higher learning, South Carolinians no longer need leave the state to find educational opportunity. In fact, an influx of talented people comes to the Midlands because it's a center of higher learning. More than twelve colleges thrive here. Their undergraduate and graduate programs attract some of the nation's top scholars, many of whom remain here.

Allen University, founded in 1870 by the African Methodist Episcopal Church, is accredited by the Commission on Colleges of the Southern Association of Colleges and Schools.

Benedict College, founded in 1870, is an independent coeducational college and one of the fastest growing of the 39 United Negro College Fund schools.

University of South Carolina, founded in 1801 as South Carolina College, offers undergraduate and graduate degrees and professional programs as well as online education. The university has earned the Carnegie Foundation's top-tier designation in research activity and community engagement. It offers 324 unique degree options to its enrollment of 31,964.

Columbia International University is Christian institution committed to "preparing men and women to know Christ and to make Him known."

Lutheran Theological Southern Seminary, founded in 1830, is a seminary of the Evangelical Lutheran Church. One of the oldest Lutheran seminaries in North America, Southern is situated atop Seminary Ridge, the highest point in the Midlands area near the geographic center of the city.

FAST-GROWING BENEDICT COLLEGE HAS THE SECOND LARGEST UNDERGRADUATE POPULATION OF SOUTH CAROLINA'S 20 PRIVATE INSTITUTIONS. BENEDICT ENCOURAGES ITS STUDENTS TO GIVE BACK TO THE COMMUNITY. ▼

Photos on pages 88-89 by Paul Ringger

Midlands Technical College, part of the South Carolina Technical College System, is a two-year, comprehensive, public, community college, offering diverse programs in career education, four-year college-transfer options, and continuing education. It is comprised of six campuses and accredited by the Commission on Colleges of the Southern Association of Colleges and Schools.

Columbia College, founded in 1854, it is one of the oldest women's colleges in the United States. The College has been ranked since 1994 by *U.S. News & World Report* as one of the top ten regional liberal arts colleges in the South.

LUTHERAN THEOLOGICAL SEMINARY, MIDLANDS TECH, COLUMBIA COLLEGE: ACADEMIC BUILDINGS ON CAMPUSES OF INSTITUTIONS OF HIGHER LEARNING BRING DIVERSE ARCHITECTURES TO THE MIDLANDS.

CLASSIC ARCHITECTURAL LINES, CAMPUS GREENSPACES, AND WATER FEATURES GIVE INSTITUTIONS OF HIGHER LEARNING A PEACEFUL YET FORMAL ATMOSPHERE CONDUCIVE TO THE PURSUIT OF KNOWLEDGE. SHOWN HERE ARE (ON THE LEFT PAGE) LENOIR-RHYNE UNIVERSITY/LUTHERAN THEOLOGICAL SOUTHERN SEMINARY, AND (ON THIS PAGE) COLUMBIA COLLEGE.

City of rivers, vistas, and dreams

While smoky blue ridges and peaks and green marshes' surging waves draw tourists to the north and south respectively, the Midlands is not hurting for beauty. *A Sense of the Midlands* (with permission from Muddy Ford Press) discussed the treasures that abound in Columbia and the Midlands. Come and let's take a leisurely stroll through the seasons in the Midlands.

In the summer, we can walk over to a Lexington County peach orchard. Treading ancient dunes we see the fine pink blossoms.

Though the coast is far away, crab cakes and shrimp and grits are not. Restaurants bring gems inland from the sea. What is more southern than a pat of butter melting in grits? Adluh Flour sits in the heart of the city and its fine products warm the hearts of diners in not just Columbia but northern cities also. Adluh produces flour, cornmeal, mixes, breaders, and feed products today—grinding wheat and yellow corn grown almost exclusively in South Carolina.

Portraits abound, historical and otherwise, in and around the city of rivers, vistas, and dreams. In early darkness a photographer stalks dawn.

When a gossamer veil of light falls upon Saluda River rapids, soft clicks capture it. Brightening, the river sings its river song. Along its banks, ferns bunch up like collards, and humus releases its earthy, uplifting fragrance, the scent of life rising from death. Across the I-126 bridges, the Broad River purls beneath a bluff where Confederate soldiers sleep.

Come cooler months, fleecy cirrus clouds stream across the sky. Winter sunsets over Lake Murray and Wateree are not to be missed.

Up near Blythewood, a plume of fragrant woodsmoke pours from a chimney; departed grandparents and old smokehouses come to mind. Sugar-cured hams, brewing coffee, and roaring fireplaces too.

Spring fetches blizzards of dogwood bracts. March winds topple trees and whitecaps sweep across lakes. Flora aplenty here. At the Governor's Mansion yellow roses twine around Doric columns, giving off a sweet fragrance.

A handsome past hides here. Old country stores stand as empty reminders of days when men in suspenders and felt hats operated charming centers of commerce.

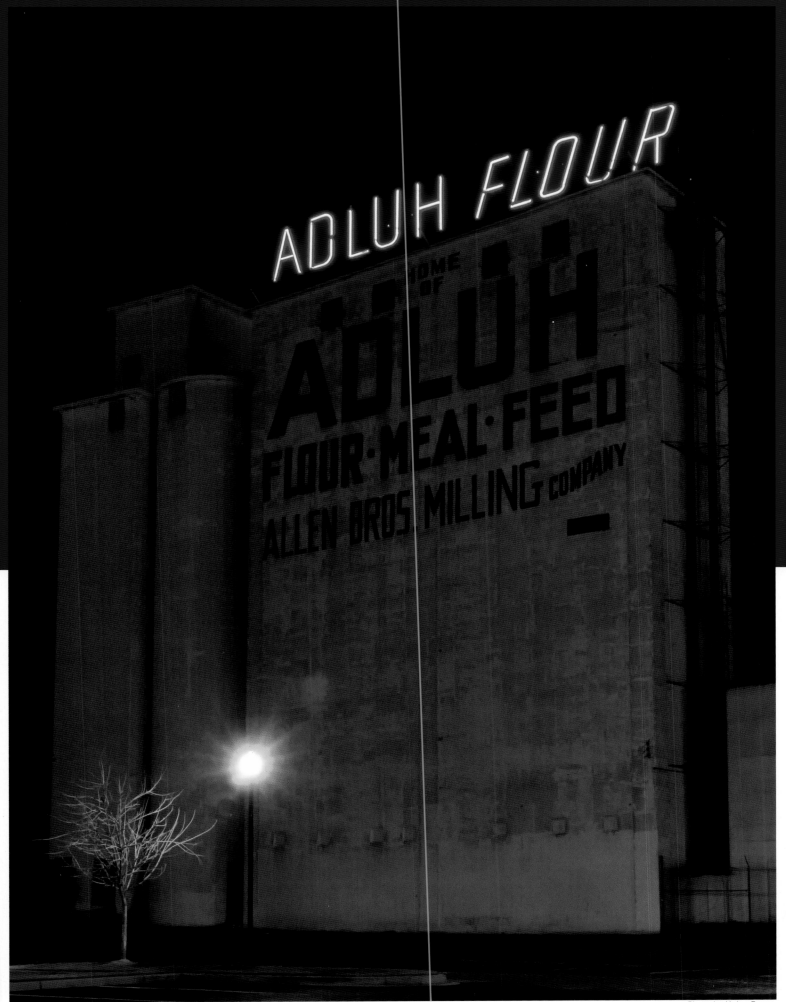

Photo by Helen Evans

City of rivers, vistas, and dreams

COLUMBIA IS A CITY WHERE WATERWAYS PULL ON PEOPLE HARD. IT WAS THAT WAY BEFORE THE AUTOMOBILE. A SETTLEMENT TOOK HOLD AND IN TIME MEN BUILT BRIDGES. EVEN THOUGH PEOPLE DRIVING ACROSS RIVERS OUTNUMBER THOSE WHO CANOE AND KAYAK THEM, NEVER FORGET THAT RIVERS BROUGHT FOLKS TO WHAT WOULD BE COLUMBIA.

Photo by Paul Ringger

COLUMBIA

On a Spanish moss-oak-shaded road in the High Hills of Santee, you will see historic sites and feel you are in the mountains and on the coast all at once. State Route 261 winds through an area that's rural, isolated, and heartbreakingly antebellum.

The columned ruins of Millwood Plantation and Saluda Factory's keystone arch impress and depress. Ruins, like music, speak to us.

One night fiddle music inspired by Appalachia floated out of a West Columbia pickin' parlor. Not far off, the Gervais Street Bridge, built in 1927-1928, evoked images of Europe, and the bridge's arches and cast iron light fixtures earn favor with artists and photographers. It was the only bridge spanning the Congaree River in Columbia until the Blossom Street Bridge went up in 1953. It was an odd but pleasing juxtaposition, this merging of Appalachia and Europe, but you would expect no less from Columbia.

Columbia and the Midlands amount to a country of rivers, sandhills, shores, and dreams. The region is blessed with the state's only national park, three rivers, and abundant charm, culture, and history. When you realize just how blessed the area is, it is easy to see why visionary leaders have worked hard to hold onto and enhance Columbia and the region's resources. Greenspaces, rivers, trails, and forests remind us that Columbia and its outlying regions abound with nature's gifts, resources not lost on leaders present and past. This appreciation for nature is a tradition.

The University of South Carolina had a president once by the name of Tom Jones. In the late 1960s when he was attempting to persuade a promising young poet to move to Columbia, he looked the poet in the eye "with sincere friendliness and said, 'If you like two things, you would like to live in South Carolina.'

'What two things,' asked the poet.

'Flowers and birds,' replied Jones.

'Talk on,' said the poet," who made Columbia his home to his dying day.

"Flowers and birds." You can say the same about Columbia, a city on the move, a famously hot city, if you will, that faces a prosperous future in a beautiful setting. If you like what you see in this transformative city, you would like to live in Columbia, South Carolina. Because if we make up a list that adds to those two wonderful things, flowers and birds, we would end up with a book as thick as the beams in the grand old Union Station.

Photo by Sam Holland

City of rivers, vistas, and dreams

M B I A

a Photo Essay

Photo by Helen Evans

COLUMBIA

Photo by Helen Evans

City of rivers, vistas, and dreams

COLUMBIA

Photo by Helen Evans

City of rivers, vistas, and dreams

Photo by Sam Holland

City of rivers, vistas, and dreams

COLUMBIA

City of rivers, vistas, and dreams

Photo by Paul Ringger

THE **T**HREE **R**IVERS **G**REENWAY OFFERS PLACES TO UNWIND, REFLECT, AND WATCH OLD MAN RIVER ROLL BY. PAGES 98-99

HIGH-RISE REFLECTIONS SHOWER DOWNTOWN **C**OLUMBIA WITH COLORED LIGHT AND ABSTRACT IMAGES. PAGES 100-101

A SUN JUST OVER THE HORIZON PAINTS TWO RIVERS' CONFLUENCE WITH THE PASTELS OF DUSK. PAGES 102-103

SOME SHOOT THE RIVER; SOME FLOAT WHERE THEY MAY, AND OTHERS TAKE A BREAK ON RIVER ROCKS. **A**LL OBEY GRAVITY'S PULL. PAGES 104-105

Photos on pages 104-105 by Paul Ringger

City of rivers, vistas, and dreams

COLUMBIA

CLIMBING UP AND INTO CARGO NETS AND ZIPLINING THROUGH TREES OVER THE SALUDA RIVER FILL ZOO PATRONS AND GUESTS WITH AN EXHILARATING RUSH AS THE 1,000-FOOT FLIGHT TURNS CLIMBERS INTO TREETOP FLIERS. THE LESS ADVENTUROUS CROSS THE FOOTBRIDGE OVER THE SALUDA RIVER TO THE ZOO'S BOTANICAL GARDEN WHERE LILIES, RUINS, AND MORE WAIT.

Photos on pages 106-107 by Paul Ringger

City of rivers, vistas, and dreams

C O L U M B I A

GORILLAS LIVE AT RIVERBANKS ZOO AS PART OF THE ASSOCIATION OF ZOOS AND AQUARIUM'S GORILLA MANAGEMENT PLAN. GUESTS AND PATRONS GET TO SEE GORILLAS AT THE GORILLA BASE CAMP. IN WILD HABITAT, GORILLAS LIVE IN BANDS RANGING FROM FIVE TO 30 INDIVIDUALS LED BY AN ADULT MALE, THE LEGENDARY SILVERBACK.

THE ZOO'S MERRY-GO-ROUND OF TIGERS, PANDA BEARS, ZEBRAS, LEOPARDS, SWANS, AND MORE TAKES KIDS ON AN UP-AND-DOWN SAFARI ALL THEIR OWN.

Photos on pages 108-109 by Paul Ringger

City of rivers, vistas, and dreams

THE NORTH-SOUTH STREETS IN THE CITY OF COLUMBIA

The north-south streets, laid out in the two mile square of the original city of Columbia in 1786, were named (except for Assembly) for generals and officers who fought in the American Revolution. Most of these were native Americans, but one was the Polish Count Pulaski.

ERECTED BY COLUMBIA COMMITTEE, NATIONAL SOCIETY COLONIAL DAMES OF AMERICA IN THE STATE OF S. C. A RICHLAND COUNTY BICENTENNIAL PROJECT 1976

The streets stay the same as change sweeps through them bringing new businesses, new signage, and greenspaces while older buildings are razed, never to return. Signs of a changing city include kayaks and banners touting Cola Town as one of the top 10 places in the country to live.

famously Hot!

THE EAST-WEST STREETS IN THE CITY OF COLUMBIA

The streets of Columbia running from east to west (with a few exceptions) were named for products important in the State's economy, for the two Taylor plantations on which the new Capital was located and for prominent individuals such as Gervais, author of the bill establishing Columbia as Capital.

Photos on pages 110-111 by Paul Ringger

City of rivers, vistas, and dreams

Photo by Paul Ringger

Photo by Stephanie Norwood

Photo by Paul Ringger

City of rivers, vistas, and dreams

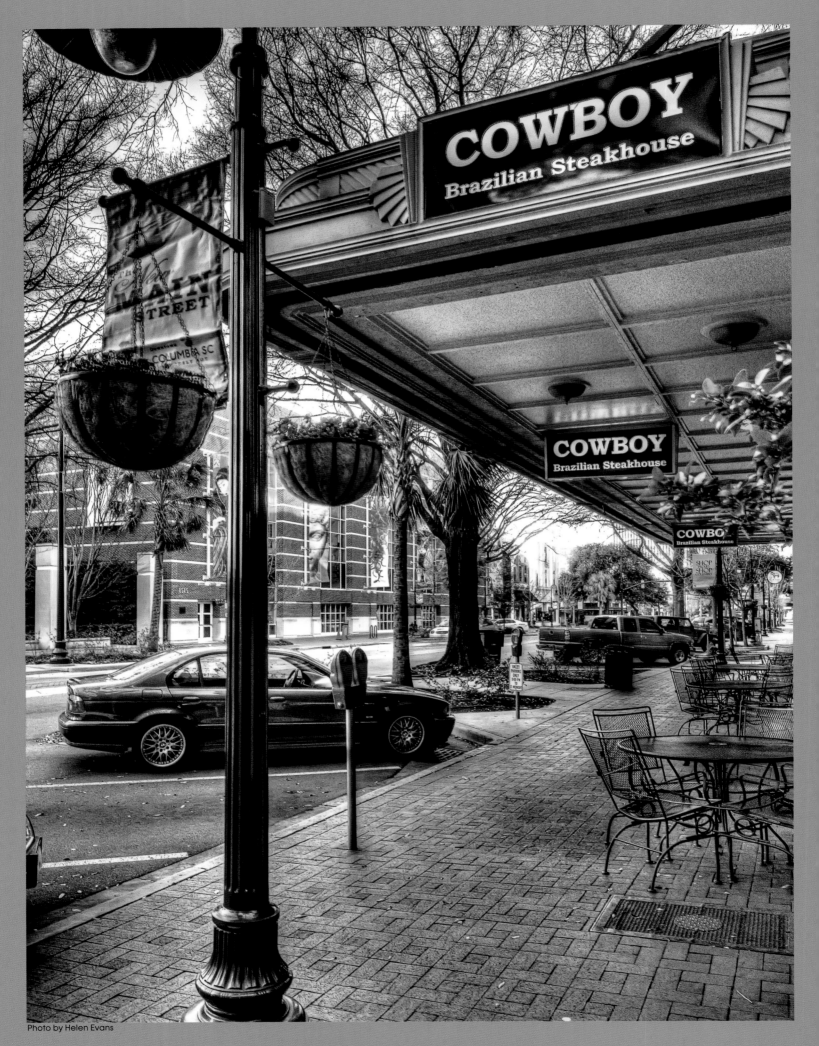

Photo by Helen Evans

COLUMBIA

Photo by Helen Evans

City of rivers, vistas, and dreams

COLUMBIA

IMPROVEMENTS TO FIVE POINTS BROUGHT WATER FEATURES TO AN AREA KNOWN, UNFORTUNATELY, FOR RAIN-INDUCED FLOODING. A LEGENDARY SITE WHERE THE BAND, HOOTIE AND THE BLOWFISH, CAME TO PROMINENCE NOW HAS A MONUMENT OF CURVED STEEL BARS SYMBOLIZING STANZAS. A GUITAR PICK SHAPED GRANITE PLAQUE BENEATH THE MONUMENT LISTS BAND MEMBERS' NAMES AND ALBUM TITLES. PAGES 112-113

IN YEARS PAST, RESTAURANTS LIKE THE ELITE EPICUREAN BROUGHT DINERS TO MAIN STREET. TODAY RESTAURANTS WITH NEW FACES AND CATCHY NAMES PLATE INTERNATIONALLY INFLUENCED ENTREES. GAUCHOS SERVE YOU AT COWBOY. IN A HURRY? TRY ONE OF THE STREET VENDORS' HOT DOGS OR SOME ITALIAN ICE. PAGES 114-115

WHEN AUTUMN'S COOL AIR SETTLES OVER FAMOUSLY HOT COLUMBIA, GUITARS, SONG, AND THE AROMA FROM GRILLS FILL THE AIR. FALL AND FESTIVALS BRING OUT THE CROWDS TO HEAR BANDS THAT PERFORM JAZZ, ROCK, BLUEGRASS, AND OTHER GENRES. PEOPLE MINGLE IN THE STREETS WHERE VENDORS HAWK DRINKS, "DOGS," FACE PAINTING, AND PLENTY OF FAMILY FRIENLDLY ACTIVITIES. THROUGHOUT THE CITY, EVENTS SUCH AS CHILI COOK OFFS, LIVE PERFORMANCES, AND ROAD RACES GIVE PEOPLE FUN WAYS TO FILL CITY STREETS. PAGES 116-117

Photos on pages 116-117 by Helen Evans

City of rivers, vistas, and dreams

Photo by Helen Evans

When football season arrives, Gamecock fever rises to, well... a feverish pitch. Cars and trucks sport flags, decals, and magnets that proclaim, "You're in Gamecock country." Throughout the Midlands, people don garnet and black and flags hang from porches. Media coverage of all things Gamecock intensifies, and Columbia resounds with rooster crows Fridays at noon.

Fans stream into the city on game days and more than 80,000 fill "The Brice." Tickets to a sold-out big game become a hot commodity.

Just before kickoff, Williams-Brice breaks into bedlam as fans twirl white towels and "Sandstorm" blasts from the speakers, whipping the crowd into a frenzy. Through losing and winning seasons Gamecock fans stick with their team.

Photos on pages 120-121 by Paul Ringger

It wasn't that long ago that Columbia's waterways were an overlooked resource. Today, people gather along riverfront parks and the canal to enjoy live music, festivals, weddings, and an assortment of community activities. Riverfront Park draws people day and night, proving that the city's waterways are now a valued asset.

City of rivers, vistas, and dreams

Photo by John Nelson

Photo by John Nelson

Over twelve October days the State Fair, one of the top 50 fairs in the country, delights thousands with its rides, food, exhibits, and competitions that celebrate South Carolina's agricultural heritage. Anyone who's been to the fair knows that "meet me at the rocket" is a phrase associated with good times ... and now and then a misplaced kid.

Photo by Tom Poland

Photo by Paul Ringger

Photo by Sam Holland

Photo by Sam Holland

C O L U M B I A

SANDY SOILS THAT CUSHION HOOVES HELPED BRING HORSE RACING TO THE MIDLANDS. FALL AND SPRING, CAMDEN'S COLONIAL AND CAROLINA CUPS RESPECTIVELY DRAW HUGE CROWDS.

IN THE PAST, COLUMBIA SPEEDWAY HOSTED RACES WHERE DRIVERS DESTINED FOR GREATNESS SUCH AS RICHARD PETTY, DAVID PEARSON, NED JARRETT, AND JUNIOR JOHNSON COMPETED. TODAY THE TRACK PROVIDES A VENUE FOR EVENTS RANGING FROM BBQ COOK-OFFS, CAR SHOWS, AND GIANT YARD SALES.

RACING IS STILL CLOSE BY THOUGH. JUST ON THE EDGE OF THE MIDLANDS SITS KERSHAW'S CAROLINA MOTORSPORTS PARK. IT'S RARE THAT A MOTORSPORTS TRACK IS MUCH CLOSER TO A CITY—EXCEPT WHERE ONE GREW UP AROUND IT. A ROUND OF THE FABULOUS AND INFAMOUS *24 HOURS OF LEMONS* IS HELD THERE ANNUALLY.

Photo courtesy of 24 Hours of LeMons

City of rivers, vistas, and dreams

Classic homes like the Seibels House and Fountains balance Columbia's more modern structures with a sense of place that speaks of a time when lots were spacious and homes revealed the influence of classic architecturural styles; times, some say, when neighborhoods were blessed with form *and* function.

Photos on pages 126-127 by Stephanie Norwood

City of rivers, vistas, and dreams

COLUMBIA'S RIVERS PROVIDE DRINK-
ING WATER, RECREATION, AND EFFLUENT
TREATMENT. COLUMBIA CANAL WATER
TREATMENT PLANT SERVES APPROXIMATELY
375,000 CUSTOMERS, MANY WHO FISH
FOR THE BIG STRIPED BASS THAT FREQUENT
THE CONGAREE RIVER. THERE WAS A TIME,
IN FACT, WHEN THE UPPER CONGAREE
BETWEEN COLUMBIA AND THE EASTMAN
KODAK PLANT PROVIDED PRIME SPAWNING
GROUNDS FOR STRIPED BASS. OUTFITTERS IN
DOWNTOWN COLUMBIA AND CITY SUBURBS
SERVE URBAN ANGLERS, TESTAMENT TO THE
CITY'S LIFE-GIVING ARTERIES' CAPACITY TO
SUSTAIN AND ENTERTAIN.

DANGER
STRONG
CURRENT
KEEP OUT

Photos on pages 128-129 by Paul Ringger

City of rivers, vistas, and dreams

RED, A WARM, PASSIONATE COLOR, OFTEN SYMBOL-
IZES LOVE AND ACCEPTANCE. A RED DOOR MEANS
"WELCOME," AN EARLY AMERICAN TRADITION THAT
TOLD TIRED TRAVELERS THEY HAD A PLACE TO STAY THE
NIGHT. THROUGHOUT THE CITY YOU'LL SEE ICONIC RED
DOORS THAT SEND MESSAGES ALL THEIR OWN: A PLACE
WHERE A DANCE CRAZE LED TO THE SOUTH CAROLINA
STATE DANCE AND DOORS THAT OPEN TO A BETTER
UNDERSTANDING OF HISTORY, ART, AND MORE. AS FOR
THE LANDMARK ADLUH FLOUR BUILDING THAT DOMI-
NATES THE VISTA, PEOPLE LOVE ITS INDUSTRIAL LOOK AND
STONE GROUND GRITS, WHICH FIND ACCEPTANCE IN
FINE RESTAURANTS HERE AND IN NEW ORLEANS.

Photos on pages 130-131 by Paul Ringger

City of rivers, vistas, and dreams

Photos on pages 132-133 by Paul Ringger

City of rivers, vistas, and dreams

Photos on pages 134-135 by Paul Ringger

City of rivers, vistas, and dreams

CROSSING THE GERVAIS STREET BRIDGE TOWARD THE STATE HOUSE, PUBLIX—ORIGINALLY THE CONFEDERATE PRINTING PLANT—SITS ON THE FAR LEFT CORNER ACROSS FROM A GREEN SPACE. EVANS & COGSWELL PRINTING COMPANY RELOCATED THE PLANT HERE FROM CHARLESTON TO AVOID SHERMAN'S WRATH, BUT TO NO AVAIL. NOW IT'S A POPULAR SUPERMARKET WHERE CANTALOUPES REPLACE CONFEDERATE BONDS. TRAINS NO LONGER RUMBLE THROUGH LINCOLN STREET, BUT THE TIRED TRACKS SERVE AS A REMINDER OF THEIR STORIED PAST. THE OLD SEABOARD DINER IS ONLY A MEMORY AND BOUTIQUES AND A STARBUCKS HAVE TAKEN UP RESIDENCE WHERE AMTRAK TRAINS ONCE GLIDED TO A STOP. BEAUTY SALONS AND BOILED PEANUT SHOPS ARE AMONG THE BUSINESSES THAT NOW CLAIM THIS STRETCH OF LINCOLN STREET, WATCHED OVER BY A PAIR OF CIGAR STORE INDIANS. PAGES 132-133

OLD AND NEW CO-EXIST IN DOWNTOWN COLUMBIA. THE LINES, TEXTURES, AND CONSTRUCTION TECHNIQUES OF YESTERYEAR AND TODAY GIVE THE CITY AN ECLECTIC CHARACTER. ASIDE FROM GOVERNMENT BUILDINGS, NO COOKIE-CUTTER, CUBE-LIKE BUILDINGS OVERDOSE THE CITY WITH BLANDNESS. MUCH OF THE CITY IS STIMULATING AND HISTORIC, DESPITE LOSSES INFLICTED BY THE FEBRUARY 18, 1865, FIREBOMBING BY THE DAMN YANKEES (ALLEGEDLY). PAGES 134-135

WHILE THE STATE HOUSE DOME READILY CATCHES THE EYE AND CAN BE SEEN FROM FAR AWAY, IT WAS NOT PART OF THE ORIGINAL BUILDING. ADDED TO THE STRUCTURE BETWEEN 1900 AND 1902, THE DOME REQUIRED 44,000 POUNDS OF COPPER TO COVER IT. THE BUILDING RECEIVED A MAJOR RENOVATION FROM 1995 TO 1998 AND NEW COPPER REPLACED THE OLD GREEN, OXIDIZED LAYER. THE RENOVATION BROUGHT THE STRUCTURE UP TO FIRE CODE AND ADDED EARTHQUAKE PROTECTION FACTORS AMONG OTHER IMPROVEMENTS. PAGES 136-137

Photo by Paul Ringger

City of rivers, vistas, and dreams

Photo by Ron Cogswell

Photo by Ron Cogswell

Photo by Paul Ringger

Photo by Ron Cogswell

THE INTERIOR OF THE STATE HOUSE IS RESPLENDENT WITH BEAUTI-
FULLY CARVED WOOD, FINE ART, AND STAINED GLASS WINDOWS.
MARBLE FLOORS, MAJESTIC COLUMNS, AND TWO GRAND
STAIRCASES.

THE FAUX DOME VISIBLE IN THE MAIN LOBBY'S CEILING SERVES AN AESTHETIC
PURPOSE ONLY. IT SHOULD NOT BE CONFUSED WITH THE ACTUAL DOME OF THE
STATE HOUSE. THE FALSE INTERIOR DOME HANGS BENEATH THE EXTERIOR DOME
OFFSET JUST ENOUGH TO BE IN THE CENTER OF THE LOBBY.

Photo by Stephanie Norwood

8

COLUMBIASALAMANDER.COM

Photo by Stephanie Norwood

BLUE SKY'S *BUSTED PLUG PLAZA* TOOK FOURTEEN MONTHS TO COMPLETE. ORIGINALLY DESIGNATED *RAINBOW DOME*, THE SCULPTURE WEIGHS 675,000 POUNDS AND CAN WITHSTAND A HIT FROM A TORNADO.

BLUE SKY'S *NEVERBUST*, A 25-FOOT WELDED STEEL CHAIN, LINKS TWO BUILDINGS ON MAIN STREET. SKY AND A CREW SECRETLY INSTALLED THE SCULPTURE, WHICH REPRESENTS POWER, ON A SUNDAY NIGHT.

YOUNG PROFESSIONALS FLOCK TO THE SHERATON'S ROOFTOP BAR WITH ITS PANORAMIC VIEW AND TO THE VISTA'S LIBERTY TAP ROOM TO DINE AND SOCIALIZE.

Photo by Paul Ringger

Photo by Stephanie Norwood

Photo by Paul Ringger

City of rivers, vistas, and dreams

PEANUTS, CHERRIES, TOMATOES ... YOU'LL FIND
THOSE AND MORE COME RAIN OR SHINE AT THE
SODA CITY FARMERS MARKET SATURDAYS FROM 9
A.M. UNTIL 1 P.M. IN THE 1500 BLOCK OF MAIN.
ETHNIC FOODS, BAKED GOODS, ARTISANS, AND
OTHER ATTRACTIONS DRAW CROWDS.

Photos on pages 142-143 by Paul Ringger

City of rivers, vistas, and dreams

THE COLUMBIA MUSEUM OF ART OPENED IN 1950 WITH A MODEST COLLECTION. TODAY IT BRINGS A CULTIVATED PRESENCE TO MAIN AND NEARBY STREETS. ITS EXHIBITIONS INCLUDE LEGENDARY ARTISTS SUCH AS NORMAN ROCKWELL AND LOCAL ARTISTS SUCH AS PHOTOGRAPHERS ROBERT CLARK AND VENNIE DEAS MOORE. AS THE MUSEUM PROCLAIMS, "TO VISIT THE CMA TODAY IS TO TAKE A JOURNEY BOTH SENSUOUS AND SPIRITUAL THROUGH WORLD HISTORY BY WAY OF THE ARTS, A JOURNEY THAT ONLY THE MOST IMAGINATIVE CREATIONS CAN MAKE POSSIBLE."

Photos on this page by Stephanie Norwood

COLUMBIASALAMANDER.COM

5

Photos on this page courtesy of the Columbia Museum of Art

City of rivers, vistas, and dreams

Photo by Paul Ringger

Photo by Stephanie Norwood

RESIDENTS AND VISITORS ENJOY THE SALLY SALAMANDER INTERACTIVE WALKING TOUR OF DOWNTOWN COLUMBIA, LINKED BY A SERIES OF NUMBERED, BRONZE CASTINGS OF A SPOTTED SALAMANDER, SOUTH CAROLINA'S STATE AMPHIBIAN.

LOCATED IN FRONT OF THE CITY OF COLUMBIA PARKING PAYMENT CENTER, *LOVELY RITA THE METER MAID* WAS CREATED FOR "CHANGE FOR CHANGE" A COMMUNITY ART PROJECT TRANSFORMING PARKING METERS INTO ART AS A FUND RAISER TO BENEFIT THE CLIMATE PROTECTION ACTION CAMPAIGN.

THE FIRST BAPTIST CHURCH (WHERE THE SECESSION CONVENTION DRAFTED A RESOLUTION ON DECEMBER 17, 1860, CREATING THE SHORT-LIVED REPUBLIC OF SOUTH CAROLINA) IS PICTURED HERE NEXT TO HIGHER GROUNDS, THE WARM, INVITING COFFEE SHOP, WHICH PROVIDES A MEETING PLACE AND EASY ACCESS TO THE CHURCH'S AMENITIES.

ORIGINALLY BUILT IN 1902, THE OLD UNION TRAIN STATION— WHICH LOOKS A BIT LIKE AN ENGLISH MANOR—IS NOW HOME TO CALIFORNIA DREAMING, A POPULAR DOWNTOWN RESTAURANT.

Photos on this page by Stephanie Norwood

City of rivers, vistas, and dreams

Photos on pages 148-149 by Paul Ringger

CHRISTOPHER COLUMBUS
1451 - 1506

A gift to Columbia, this
monument stands in tribute
to the courageous spirit of
that Genoese mariner who
challenged the unknown to
discover this land, now the
hope of the world and the
haven of freedom for all.

City of rivers, vistas, and dreams

Photo by Ron Cogswell

WHICH PLACE FOR LUNCH? MAIN STREET OFFERS APPEALING CHOICES RANGING FROM FINE DINING TO SANDWICHES.

Photo by Tom Poland

Photo by Stephanie Norwood

City of rivers, vistas, and dreams

Photos on pages 152-153 by Paul Ringger

Not far from where Harden Street runs into Rosewood sits an old-timey burger joint, a refreshing break from the cookie-cutter franchises.

A walk around Five Points takes you past fountains and well-known eateries such as Groucho's, where in 1941, Harold "Groucho" Miller began serving the recipes for potato salad, cole slaw, and sandwich dressings he had learned growing up in a Philadelphia orphanage.

City of rivers, vistas, and dreams

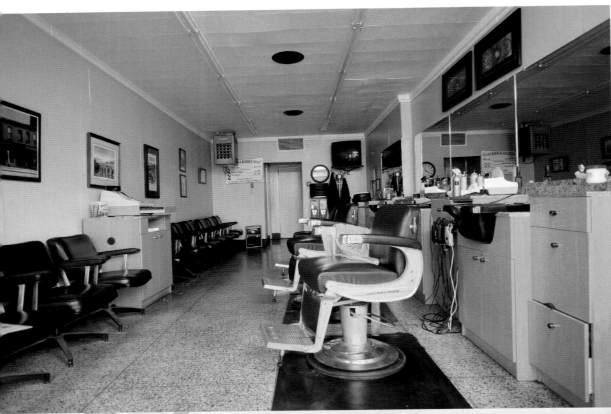

PLACES IN COLUMBIA TAKE YOU
BACK IN TIME ... AN OLD-FASHION
BARBERSHOP AND OLD THEATERS.
TURN YOUR IMAGINATION LOOSE AND
RECALL A RAZOR SLAPPING LEATHER
AND THE FRAGRANCE OF TALC AND
HAIR TONIC ... OLD FLICKERING FILMS
WITH SCRATCH LINES RUNNING DOWN
A SCREEN ... OVER ON MAIN "THE
NICK" SHOWS INDEPENDENT FILMS.

Photos on pages 148-149 by Paul Ringger

DEDICATED IN MARCH OF 2001, A PANORAMIC MONUMENT ON STATE HOUSE GROUNDS PAYS HOMAGE TO AFRICAN-AMERICANS' EPIC STRUGGLE FOR EQUAL RIGHTS. ED DWIGHT CREATED THE MONUMENT OF BRONZE AND GRANITE. SAID DWIGHT, "IT DEPICTS THE HISTORY OF AFRICAN-AMERICANS FROM THE 1619 SLAVE AUCTION BLOCKS IN CHARLESTON, TO PRESENT DAY SOUTH CAROLINA. ITS CENTRAL FEATURE IS A MAP OF THE *MIDDLE PASSAGE* WHERE ROUGHLY FORTY PERCENT OF THE SLAVES FROM AFRICA WENT DIRECTLY INTO CHARLESTON HARBOR. THE ENTRY FEATURES FOUR *RUBBING STONES* FROM THE FOUR MAIN COASTAL AREAS OF AFRICA: GHANA, SIERRA LEONE, SENEGAL, AND THE CONGO."

On the signs in the relief: **FRE & EQU**, **WE DESERVE EQUAL RIGHTS**

Photo by Ron Cogswell

Photo by Paul Ringger

MBIA

Profiles in Excellence

Biographies of the organizations whose generous support of this work made it possible.

Biographies of organizations appear in the book in the order in which they were established in Columbia.

Seibels Insurance Technology & Services
A Heritage of Quality. A Future of Excellence.

In 1869, four years after Sherman ransacked Columbia and left a charred city in his wake, Edwin W. Seibels opened a small sales operation in the city's fire-ravaged business district. The son of German immigrants, Seibels would prove to be an entrepreneur. He and Virginian James B. Ezell founded a modest fire and life insurance company that first operated out of

the back of a clothing store. Soon, the Columbia's Daily Phoenix described it as "Some of the best fire and life insurance companies in the U.S." The Seibels legacy had begun.

Over the past 150 years, Seibels Insurance Technology & Services evolved into a prominent insurance services provider known for insurance and technology expertise and a penchant for inventing and improving information management technology. Consider the company's revolutionary innovation, the vertical file cabinet.

Edwin G. Seibels' Idea—A Better Way To Manage Information

In 1891, Edwin W. Seibels' son, Edwin Grenville Seibels, developed the vertical file, a documents organization resource used worldwide today. He found the old system of placing claims papers and correspondence flat in a box clumsy and wasteful. Placing correspondence vertically in long boxes made more sense, and, in time he persuaded the Globe Files Company to construct five oak boxes, 35 inches long, 13 ½ inches wide, and 13 inches high with a roll top like that of an old-time desk. These five boxes, Seibels noted with obvious pride 40 years later, contained all the files that once occupied an entire office wall.

In 1938, the Smithsonian Institute asked Seibels to place an original box in its collection of business artifacts. On June 16, 1941, in the presence of a gathering of notables, Seibels officially presented one of his five oak boxes to the Smithsonian. The rest is history, a history that's part of Seibels' proud story of innovative information management.

Seibels has, as well, a penchant for reinventing itself. Today, Seibels Insurance Technology & Services provides Processing, Technology, and Claims Solutions to the property and casualty insurance industry. What hasn't been reinvented is the company's commitment to quality customer service, strong client relations, continuous innovation, and integrity that has been there from the start.

Solutions

Seibels backs its Processing, Technology, and Claims Solutions with a strong combination of insurance and technology expertise that helps insurers achieve maximum operational efficiency.

Business Process Outsourcing

When Seibels runs carriers back office operations, they have more time to focus on growth and productivity. Seibels professionals tailor business process services to fit their clients' needs—from underwriting and customer service to accounting and claims administration. In conjunction with its technology services, Seibels provides solutions they need to operate

–Photo by Richard Carson

effectively and efficiently. Among the company's BPO services are the following:

- Financial Services
- Accounting and Reporting
- Rating and Underwriting
- Policy Administration
- Billings and Collections
- Claims Administration
- 24/7 Customer Service Center [Bilingual English & Spanish staff]

Seibels also provides processing solutions for Coastal Market carriers' unique needs. The company's Take-Out program helps new and existing carriers acquire Florida policyholders through the Citizens Depopulation Program. Seibels helps carriers manage workloads and provides speed to market and cost-efficient operations.

Seibels Professional Services meet each carrier's unique needs—from comprehensive product maintenance and support to assistance in managing their processing environment.

TECHNOLOGY SOLUTIONS

Seibels has a heritage of technological innovation. In 1966 the company automated its policy and claims functions. By 1974, Seibels policy administration system was the first commercially available system for carriers. Today, Seibels provides the property and casualty insurance industry advanced systems. Powerful and intelligent yet flexible and innate, Seibels web-based systems manage all processing needs. Built with a strong infrastructure that adheres to industry standards, the Seibels systems help carriers' business operations flow seamlessly.

CLAIMS SOLUTIONS

Seibels full-service claims organization offers complete property and casualty claims

administration. As technology and insurance experts, the Seibels team understands claims processes from all angles. They know, too, that costs rise when claims unnecessarily remain open. Seibels Claims Solutions simplifies claims handling, improves loss ratios and customer service, and decreases loss-adjusting expenses.

With regional and national experience, Seibels Insurance Technology & Services is skilled at serving diverse carriers and risk managers. Talented specialists design solutions that reduce claims handling time and costs. Flexible and adaptable, they tailor services—bundled or unbundled—that meet clients' objectives.

COLUMBIA'S OLDEST BUSINESS

Seibels takes great pride in being a long-standing member of Columbia and the Midlands. Approximately 300 people are employed in the company's Columbia office, which sits in the historical district. Community-minded, Seibels takes pleasure in supporting local charities, with particular support for the Cystic Fibrosis Foundation.

While the company has evolved and prospered nearly 150 years, Seibels' roots have remained firmly planted in Columbia. In fact, Seibels is the oldest business enterprise within the capital city and has long had the prestigious Post Office Box One mailing address.

The secret to Seibels' longevity? Never forgetting that promises, services, reliability, trust, and loyalty mean everything.

Those core principals have distinguished Seibels Insurance Technology & Services. Though the company provides services primarily in the Southeast United States, Seibels also serves Hawaii and California. The company also maintains an office in Altamonte Springs, Florida.

The Seibels identity is firm: knowledgeable and experienced insurance professionals who provide services and technology to the property and casualty insurance industry. To learn more about Seibels' and how Seibels' Solutions can improve your business, go online and visit www.seibels.com.

▲ The Seibels trade show booth being previewed and tested at company headquarters.
–Photo by Andy Banco

◀ Photo opposite, top—Always innovative, Edwin G. Seibels invented the vertical filing system, which revolutionized file management.

◀▼ Part entrance, part gallery: the Seibels lobby welcomes guests with a tour of the company's history.

Constructed in 1950 in the International Style, the Seibels building is a well-known Columbia landmark. ▼

–Photo by Andy Banco

South Carolina State Fair

Promoting Agriculture, Industry, and Education

The guns of the American Civil War had fallen silent for only four years when a group of forward thinking South Carolinians sought to resurrect two agricultural societies that had sponsored fairs in the Palmetto State between 1836 and Secession in 1861. As the South underwent Reconstruction after the War, this group realized that for South Carolina

▲ *The Worm Ride is a popular mid-way treat for young and old.*

to grow and prosper during this era they would need to expand their focus beyond only agricultural programs. The State Agricultural and Mechanical Society of South Carolina was founded in 1869 by these visionaries, many of whom were former members of the pre-war agricultural societies. With a new constitution, "the object of which shall be to develop and promote the entire material interests of the State," they were ready to look to the future.

The new group faced the challenge of starting literally from the ground up. General William Sherman's army had burned the former Society's fair buildings in 1865. The South Carolina state legislature would lend a hand with a $2,500 appropriation to assist the Society in launching its initiative.

A diversification from almost total reliance on the agrarian based economy of the state was needed. The Society began sponsoring fairs that introduced new exhibits and programs on how South Carolina could accomplish this diversification. Columbia enjoys the enviable position of being in the geographic center of the state. While there had also been a South Carolina Industrial Fair in Charleston prior to the War, it had never been as well attended as the Columbia event because of poor transportation facilities. By 1869, Columbia had developed into a railroad hub and traveling to the state's capital city was easy for citizens from across South Carolina. In addition, the city provided both the site for the fair as well as funds to help construct the necessary facilities.

From 1869 through 1903 the South Carolina State Fair was located on Elmwood Avenue in downtown Columbia. In 1904 the site was moved away from downtown to Rosewood Drive where it remains today. The grounds are comprised of six exhibit halls, an administrative office building, a meeting and fair support building, and assorted animal barns and arenas. The Fair also has a 4,000 space landscaped parking lot.

A FAIR FOR THE 21ST CENTURY

The South Carolina State Fair continues to keep its very important agricultural roots alive, while offering fun, food, education and great competitive exhibit opportunities for all. Each October, people of all ages come to Columbia to enjoy the exhibits as well as livestock competitions. Exciting live entertainment showcases a broad range of musical genres.

The South Carolina State Fairgrounds is a year round meeting, trade show, and activity facility that is a self-supporting, not-for-profit entity. It is not owned or funded by any government agency. Each year, the South Carolina State Fair awards $300,000 in scholarships for post-secondary education to fifty students across the state. In addition, the Fair hosts the annual region-wide free Medical Mission at no charge for the United Way and major hospitals in the area. It also donates thousands of dollars annually to region-wide charities such as the Salvation Army, Harvest Hope Food Bank, and others.

The South Carolina State Fair today operates with a full-time management and operations staff of twenty-one people. During the annual Fair, the part-time paid staff expands to more than 600.

Patrons and exhibitors from every county in the state and

The colorful Ellison Carousel features creatures beyond the traditional horses. ▼

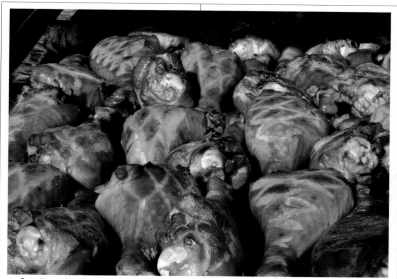

▲ Smoky turkey legs are just one of the many tasty treats available to fair-goers.

▲ Equestrian competitions are an annual highlight.

visitors from neighboring Georgia and North Carolina comprise an annual crowd of approximately 500,000. In addition, trade shows held at the Fairgrounds during the year draw a client base from states across the country.

The most famous landmark on the fairgrounds is "The Rocket", a Jupiter medium-range ballistic missile designed by Dr. Werner Von Braun. Deployed in Italy and Turkey in 1961 as part of NATO's Cold War deterrent against the Soviet Union, the rocket, formerly named the Columbia, was given to the Capital City by the U.S. Air Force.

The South Carolina State Fair is now the largest event in the state and ranks thirty-seventh in attendance among the over 1,000 fairs held annually in the United States.

GIVING BACK TO THE COMMUNITY

Over the years, the Fair has been recognized on numerous occasions for its contributions to the community. Among the most appreciated was the 2011 President's Award from the Columbia Urban League for the Fair's commitment to education. For seventeen years, the South Carolina State Fair "Ride of Your Life" Scholarship Program has helped launch bright futures for deserving students in the state. The Fair is excited to continue this tradition by awarding these scholarships to deserving students again in 2014.

"We take very seriously our obligation to promote the material, educational, agricultural, and industrial interest of our State," noted Bill Cantey, President of the Fair's Executive Committee. "We will continue to improve our facilities and operations in the future as South Carolina moves forward."

The midway's giant Ferris Wheel provides a breath-taking view of the Fair as well as thrills for the riders.. ▼

RICHLAND
LIBRARY
access freely.

access · freely.

Photo by Paul Ringer

1431

Richland Library

Providing Resources and Services to Richland County

With eleven convenient locations across Richland County and a satellite location at Edventure Children's Museum, Richland Library is a vibrant, contemporary organization that provides resources and services that help people find jobs, get ready for and succeed in school, and access technology and resources for learning and leisure. As the center of the

community, Richland Library has accepted the challenges of serving people in the digital age.

The role of libraries everywhere has changed drastically in recent years. Libraries are no longer just about books, but about learning and providing opportunities for all people to come together, create and share with others. Richland Library has kept pace with our rapidly changing world and has adapted its resources and their accessibility to the people of Richland County.

Richland Library is all about access – access to information and resources. Traditional offerings – children's books, popular fiction and nonfiction, music CDs and movies – are still in high demand, but the library is also bridging the digital divide and ensuring access to electronic resources and devices for everyone. As highlighted in the *Wall Street Journal*, availability and

usage of the library's eResources (eBooks, downloadable music and more) have skyrocketed.

- More than 24,300 customers are registered to use the library's eBook services.
- More than 215,000 music downloads completed in only two years, averaging 9,000 downloads and 1,420 users each month.
- More than 4,000 customers are now accessing the 300+ eMagazine titles available, averaging 16,000 checkouts each month. Approximately 200 customers monthly are discovering this service which was launched in December 2013.

In addition, Richland Library offers numerous outreach services and partnerships; outstanding collections in multiple formats; and more than 4,600 programs that reach over 84,000 people of all ages each year. Library locations were visited more than 2.7 million times in 2013 and checked out more than 5.2 million items. Upwards of 8,000 people each day are served at the library's eleven locations. Wireless access is

provided to more than 100,000 customers each year. The library's website www.richlandlibrary.com, had more than 2.3 million visits in 2013. And Richland's meeting room use experienced a 56 percent increase during that same time period.

Accessibility to its resources remains a high priority with the library's staff. Each month, one staff person and two volunteers deliver more than 1,000 books to 175 library customers who can no longer physically visit the library. The visits and the books become a vital resource for these customers, who eagerly await the next visit from the library.

"This is an exciting time for Richland Library," states Melanie Huggins, Richland Library's Executive Director. "We're passionate about learning and sharing resources that keep our community healthy and vibrant. The way people use the library has certainly changed dramatically, but the services we provide are more important today than ever before."

▲ The number of Richland Library cardholders who used their library cards within the past year would max out capacity at the University of South Carolina Williams Brice Stadium.

◄ Offering state-of-the-art technology, Richland Library provides a truly customizable, modern library experience for residents and visitors alike.

◄▼ Teens can connect their personal interests, peer learning and academics to create a sweet spot of meaningful learning in the library's Teen Center at Richland Library Main in downtown Columbia.

▼ Stay connected with free Wi-Fi at any of the library's 11 locations, or popular Wi-Fi hot spots sprinkled throughout the county.

Nelson Mullins Riley & Scarborough LLP

From a silver coffee pot to a thriving law firm

But for a silver coffee pot, Nelson Mullins Riley & Scarborough LLP may never have existed. In 1872, Patrick Henry Nelson was 16 years old and ready to attend college, but in the destitute times of post-Civil War South Carolina, his parents did not have the funds for higher education. Patrick's mother, however, was determined. The Nelsons' only item of value was a

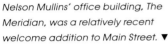

Tiffany coffee pot, which she sold to pay for her son's tuition at Sewanee. The coffee pot paid dividends because Pat Nelson went on to become a lawyer, and in 1897, he moved his practice to Columbia and founded the firm that grew from one lawyer to more than 500 lawyers and other professionals practicing in 14 offices, including offices in the District of Columbia,

Nelson Mullins' office building, The Meridian, was a relatively recent welcome addition to Main Street. ▼

privacy and security, white collar crime, and other needs of clients. Nelson Mullins lawyers have handled cases in most states in the United States and have argued before many appellate courts. Nelson Mullins' clients range from Fortune 500 companies to venture-backed and emerging enterprises to start ups, as well as individuals, non-profit entities, and

SOUTH CAROLINA ROOTS.

Even though it has grown significantly, Nelson Mullins maintains deep roots in South Carolina, with its largest office in Columbia, as well as offices in Greenville, Myrtle Beach, and Charleston. In addition to its attorneys, Nelson Mullins has more than 500 staff employees in South

The portraits of certain of the name partners of Nelson Mullins remind the Firm's attorneys of its history. ►▲

Florida, Georgia, Massachusetts, North Carolina, South Carolina, Tennessee and West Virginia.

BREADTH OF SERVICES.

The attorneys at Nelson Mullins provide advice and counsel to its corporate and individual clients in a wide variety of areas, including litigation, corporate, banking, economic development, securities, finance, tax, estate planning, intellectual property, governmental relations, regulatory, healthcare, environmental, real estate, labor and employment,

trusts. Because of the varied experiences of its attorneys and other professionals, Nelson Mullins' professionals are able to draw upon the knowledge and experience of other professionals throughout the Firm to serve its clients. Nelson Mullins also has a document management and e-discovery division named Encompass that provides electronic discovery, document review, and information governance services to its clients.

Carolina. Keeping many of its staff jobs in South Carolina not only helps the South Carolina economy but also makes economic sense for the Firm and its clients.

LEADERSHIP.

Nelson Mullins and its lawyers are leaders in their chosen practices, industries, and local communities. William Hubbard, who practices in the Columbia office, is the current President of the American Bar Association. Other Nelson Mullins lawyers include four past presidents of DRI

– The Voice of the Defense Bar and three past presidents and the current president of Lawyers for Civil Justice. Nelson Mullins has also had several of its partners serve as president of the South Carolina Bar, including most recently Marvin Quattlebaum in 2011-2012.

Nelson Mullins professionals include a former U.S. Secretary of Education and former Governor of South Carolina, a former Lt. Governor of North Carolina, two former U.S. Ambassadors, former members of Congress, a former

A LAW FIRM WITH A HEART.

Nelson Mullins is committed to serving the public welfare. The firm handles complex pro bono litigation, corporate matters, and legislative advocacy, as well as individual pro bono representation. In 1992 Nelson Mullins earned the ABA's Pro Bono Publico Award, given annually to law firms for extraordinary contributions in providing legal services to the poor and disadvantaged. Nelson Mullins became a charter member of the Pro Bono Challenge of the Pro Bono Institute in 1993. In

service including seven attorneys who have been recipients of the South Carolina Bar Pro Bono Lawyer of the year award.

The firm has sponsored externships and fellowships with several agencies, including the Atlanta Legal Aid Society, the South Carolina Appleseed Legal Justice Center, and the South Carolina Center for Capital Litigation. Two programs of the firm include Wills for Heroes (in which the firm's volunteers have provided thousands of free wills to first responders throughout South Carolina, North

The lobby in Nelson Mullins' Columbia office provides a great view of Columbia and the Capitol Building. ▼

Chair of the U.S. Consumer Product Safety Commission, and other government and community leaders. In addition, firm partners have chaired the boards of three South Carolina colleges: William Hubbard at the University of South Carolina (and John von Lehe currently serves as Chair-Elect), David Wilkins at Clemson University, and John Moore at Erskine College.

2005 the firm received the John Minor Wisdom Public Service and Professionalism Award from the Litigation Section of the American Bar Association and the William B. Spann, Jr. Award from the State Bar of Georgia, that organization's highest pro bono honor. In 2013 the National Legal Aid & Defender Association selected Nelson Mullins to receive a Beacon of Justice Award for providing pro bono representation to those unable to afford representation. Many individual firm attorneys have also been recognized for their dedication to pro bono

Carolina, and Georgia) and the recently launched Lawyers 4 Vets (a free legal clinic for lower-income veterans).

A GREAT PLACE TO CALL HOME.

Nelson Mullins is very fortunate to have been founded in Columbia and to be able to remain an active member of its community. Columbia has provided our professionals and staff a great place to live, work, play, and raise our families. We are proud to call Columbia home.

Columbia Chamber

A Strong Voice for the Columbia Region

The population of Columbia had barely topped 21,000 in 1902 when the organization that would become the Columbia Chamber first opened its doors. Immediately immersing itself in the business of promoting the city, the Chamber's earliest efforts included backing a proposal to establish a permanent Army post in the area, calling for the elimination of tolls on local bridges, and helping to bring the South Atlantic States Corn Exposition to Columbia in 1910. Over the next century, the Columbia Chamber would evolve into a strong voice with a singular mission - promoting not only the City of Columbia, but also businesses enterprises, civic organizations, educational institutions, and individuals in Calhoun, Fairfield, Kershaw, Lexington, Newberry, and Richland Counties.

The Columbia Chamber serves as the voice of its partners and the business community at large on matters of economic, educational, social, cultural and political concern. In addition, the Chamber supports and promotes the success of its partners through networking, professional development, advocacy and leadership. The organization's fifteen full-time and one part-time employees strive to make the Columbia region the most economically prosperous in the United States. They work diligently to fulfill the Chamber's promise to connect, engage, impact and transform the region.

Fulfilling that promise requires working together as a community to accomplish the following goals:

- Creating a regional vision and plan
- Continuing to build support for local military installations
- Cultivating a competitive business climate for the Midlands
- Establishing and maintaining strong relationships with local, state and federal government
- Partnering with local institutions of higher education and technical colleges to ensure a competitive workforce
- Supporting the progress and continuing development of local infrastructure and transportation needs

A Century of Growth and Service

The visionaries who founded the Columbia Chamber were acutely aware of the region's many amenities. Situated in the geographical center of South Carolina where three major rivers converge, the Columbia area rippled with opportunity since the city's founding in 1786. Columbia grew to become the capital of the Palmetto State as well as its largest city. Recognizing the great growth potential for the city, the early Chamber partners touted the myriad attractions of the area to businesses and individuals seeking to locate in the area that boasted a mild climate and a regional hub of transportation. In 1915, after just thirteen years in operation, the diligence of the Chamber's leaders helped attract a Harvest Jubilee and State Fair that drew 100,000 people who spent more than a half-million dollars (1915 dollars!) in Columbia.

That same diligence continued to attract people and businesses to the area over the years. In addition, the Chamber's reputation for success in everything from supporting public works improvements to building strong relationships with governmental agencies led to rapid growth as the organization's partnership rolls increased.

By the 1930s, as the nation and the world languished in the Great Depression, the efforts of the Columbia Chamber resulted in attracting new industries to Columbia. An aggressive

▲ *Carl Blackstone, President & CEO.*

▼ *Business Professionals of the Year are honored at Annual Gala & Auction.*

nationwide campaign led by the Chamber resulted in a Veterans Hospital locating in Columbia and the attraction of numerous out-of-town businesses through the production of the area's first industrial brochure. The Chamber maintained a tight focus on the city's slogan of "City Unlimited" as Columbia celebrated its 150th anniversary in 1936.

Those efforts and the tireless work of subsequent leaders of the Columbia Chamber have resulted today in a dynamic organization that continues to tout the attributes of the Columbia area, now home to a diverse population of more than 700,000 people. The Chamber takes great pride in helping to create and promote an environment where businesses can flourish. Working on behalf of more than 1,500 partners, the Chamber provides an integrated series of programs and services that help the community's businesses, individuals, educational institutions, and civic organizations thrive and grow.

Today's Columbia Chamber

Led by a Board of Directors composed of dedicated volunteers, the Columbia Chamber today operates as a private, non-profit, partnership-driven organization that unites the voices of more than 1,500 partners from across the business spectrum. An Executive Committee from the Board sets policy direction and governs the Chamber's operations.

The advantages that Chamber partnership offers have expanded greatly over its more than a century of service to the city and the region. Serving as the voice of its partners and the business community at large on matters of economic, educational, cultural and political concern, the Chamber also supports and promotes the success of its partners through networking, professional development, advocacy and leadership. The broad

range of initiatives spearheaded by the Chamber are a joint effort between Midlands businesses and many local municipal, economic development and community entities with the shared vision of building a strong future for all Midlands residents.

Boundless opportunities now exist for partners to learn and grow. From volunteer activities to time-honored traditions, Columbia Chamber partners have a never-ending path toward personal and professional growth through a host of programs and events to enjoy throughout the year:

COR

Columbia Opportunity Resource (COR) connects talented professionals with opportunities for leadership, service and fun. More than 160 guests learned how to lead, give back and engage in Columbia at CORrelate, COR's annual celebration. In addition, COR participated in the first Midlands Gives in 2013, raising $6,325 and ranking seventh out of

149 organizations for number of unique donors.

IT Council

In 2013, the Chamber hosted more than 500 IT professionals at IT Council educational luncheons. In addition to hosting a

▲ *Partners enjoy the Annual Golf Tournament.*

▼ *Chamber honors South Carolina Teachers of the Year.*

▲ *Partners are invited to network and get involved at Business@ Midday.*

▶▲ *IT Council honors community information technology leaders.*

Military Appreciation Night at the Blowfish Game. ▶▼

▼ *Save Our Fort Petition to Support Fort Jackson.*

representative from Microsoft, IT Council collaborated with other organizations, including POSSCON, SCITDA, CTC, ConvergeSC, and ConnectSC.

SMALL AND MINORITY BUSINESS FOCUS

The Chamber's popular "Business Spotlight Recognition" program recognizes Columbia area small businesses for their excellence in specified categories including diversity and community contributions. Also popular are Chamber-sponsored workshops designed to assist small, minority and women owned businesses in their quest to survive and expand in today's challenging economy.

MILITARY AFFAIRS

The Columbia Chamber has a long tradition of promoting the greater Columbia region as the most military friendly community in America through a broad range of activities, meetings, recognition, and promotions. They are very much aware of nearby Fort Jackson's importance to the Columbia area with 7,000 direct jobs and 12,000 dependents. Chamber staff coordinate bi-monthly meetings of the Military Affairs Committee, attended regularly by more than 60 partners. They are also active in coordinating the "Hiring our Heroes" employment fair that in 2013 brought together more than 85 employers, 1,200 veterans, and

media coverage by all local media. From developing active grassroots initiatives to provide feedback to the Secretary of the Army on Fort Jackson's economic impact on the Columbia area to coordinating Military Appreciation/Ike Night at the Blowfish Stadium with the Blowfish staff and Fort Jackson attended by 3,000 soldiers, the Columbia Chamber sets a high priority on initiatives and programs that focus on Columbia's reputation as a military friendly community.

PUBLIC POLICY

Chamber staff strongly support the organization's Legislative Agenda and provide information

to its partners to enlist their assistance on matters of public policy, including working with the state legislature to pass military friendly legislation.

These and numerous other Chamber programs and initiatives resulted in partnership doubling during the 2012-2013 calendar year as the Chamber welcomed more than 400 new partners to its ranks.

LEADING THE CHAMBER IN THE 21ST CENTURY

Leading the Columbia Chamber today is Carl Blackstone, the President and CEO of the organization. Selected by the Board of Directors after

the passing of Ike McLeese, who had held the position for nineteen years, Blackstone brings an extensive background in public policy, government relations, and strategic communications along with a wealth of experience working with small and large businesses and trade associations of all levels. He assumed the position with an infectious enthusiasm that would identify his leadership style in steering an organization that is highly regarded in the area.

"I realize that many challenges lie ahead, and I hope to play a pivotal role in the business community and make the same impact that identified my predecessor," Blackstone noted. "Moving forward, the Columbia Chamber

will continue to expand its effort to encourage cooperation among geographic areas, political entities, governments and other stakeholders that have direct impact on the processes that add strength to programs for improving our community. Understanding the culture, creating familiarity, building and using a common language, agreeing on specific actions and ultimately sharing work and risks are essential to generating proper momentum to move our region forward."

▲ *Leadership Columbia celebrates their class project with a ribbon cutting.*

◄▲ *City of Columbia and Richland County proclaim Small Business Week.*

▼ *Working to find Veterans jobs with Hiring Our Heroes.*

Photo by Paul Ringger

Seastrunk Electric Company, Inc.

Electrical Contractors Since 1927

▲ *The company relocated from Main Street to its present location on Harden Street in 1941.*

More than 80 years ago, F. Jack Seastrunk founded an electrical contracting business on Main Street in the heart of downtown Columbia. Seastrunk Electric Company has been in continuous operation since that time and is still lighting Columbia today.

The company quickly grew and expanded its scope of services to the point that Seastrunk was the company the War Department (today's Department of Defense) turned to during World War II. Seastrunk was selected to provide high voltage lines to numerous military facilities not only in South Carolina, but as far away as Florida and Texas. During the war years, the work that Seastrunk completed at what was then "Camp" Jackson helped the Army post grow to become Fort Jackson, a prominent player in the area's economy today.

Following the war, Seastrunk's line crews continued to work with the military until 1955 when the company's business focus shifted and the project manager heading that department retired. A returning World War II veteran would join the company as a warehouse employee in 1945. After almost 20 years of service, John Slice would become a co-owner. Slice joined Eddie Seastrunk in owning and operating Seastrunk Electric when the

▶▼ *Second and third generation owners, Eddie and Edwin Seastrunk, estimating a pending project.*

▼ *Seastrunk Electric on Main Street, circa 1930.*

founder retired in 1963 and sold the company.

A Family Tradition

Members of the Slice and Seastrunk families would continue to walk in their fathers' footsteps over the years as electrical contractors. John Slice would receive his "Master of Trade" designation and saw his son, Grady, join the ranks. Learning the business from the ground up, Grady had worked with Seastrunk Electric since he was in high school and became a full-time employee after serving in the military. Grady retired after many years as a Senior Project Manager.

Eddie Seastrunk and his brothers, Bobby and Charles, worked for Seastrunk Electric during their college years. Graduating from Newberry College in 1956, Eddie became full-time in the business as an estimator before becoming co-owner seven years later. A third generation of the family remains active with the business today as Edwin

Seastrunk joined the company after attending college. Eddie Seastrunk's primary role today is that of estimator while Edwin handles the daily operations.

"We've been involved with many projects over the years, and they vary in size and range," Eddie Seastrunk states. "We have worked on hospitals, schools, churches, and office buildings. Our most recent projects have included renovations to the Woodrow Wilson Family Home, Garners Ferry Road Adult Activity Center, and the new education center at St. Martin In the Fields Episcopal Church. We were also recently selected to be the electrical contractor in the expansion of First Community Bank with its opening of a downtown branch on Lady Street. Seastrunk Electric was the electrical contractor on this building when it was built in 1964 and we were the company they turned to a half-century later. We are very proud to be continuing the tradition of excellence that has identified Seastrunk Electric since 1927."

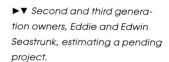

The Arnold Companies
Embracing the Entrepreneurial Spirit

The year was 1907. Newspaper headlines were trumpeting the admission of Oklahoma as the 46th state in the Union and the grand opening of a previously unknown department store named Neiman-Marcus in Dallas, Texas. While there were no headlines anywhere of 14-year old Ben Arnold selling candy, cigars, and the Wall Street Journal on a ferryboat in Florida, that teenager with a passion for becoming an entrepreneur began pursuing a dream that future members of his family continue to build on today.

Arnold went on to found a liquor distribution business after the end of Prohibition in 1933. His son, Norman J. Arnold, expanded his father's business into the largest spirits wholesaler in South Carolina before selling the operation in 1984.

The founder's grandson, Ben D. Arnold, was himself bitten by the entrepreneurial bug after graduation from the University of Florida in 1989 with degrees in finance and real estate. While interning with a real estate developer, Ben realized that he was drawn to that field and decided to launch his own career as a property tax consultant. Arnold quickly displayed the same entrepreneurial acumen that identified his father and grandfather. Operating with a single laptop computer in a room of his apartment, Arnold grew his business to the point that his company was handling tax appeals on $1 billion in assessed value of commercial and residential real estate throughout the Southeast in the early 1990s.

Ben Arnold's "boots on the ground" experience and hard-won expertise led him to partner with his father in founding the Arnold Family Corporation, a property development and management company, in 1994, one of the most diverse owners and developers of commercial and multi-family properties in the Southeast. The company also specializes in designing and building properties that vary from traditional commercial real estate to mixed-use entertainment complexes to neo-traditional town centers, elderly housing, and marinas.

Two Decades of Growth

Arnold Family Corporation today is headquartered in Columbia and leases and manages approximately three-quarters of a million square feet of office, warehouse, and retail space throughout South Carolina. Operating as a full-service real estate management firm, the company provides property management to a wide array of commercial properties, including professional offices, retail, restaurant, entertainment, industrial, and warehouse properties. Included in the company's portfolio are some of the most recognized landmarks in the region:

▲ *The Palms on Main tropical pool in Downtown Columbia.*

The Palms on Main Front Entrance. ▼

The Palms on Main view from Main Street, with ground floor retail and restaurants, and a view of the Stephen Gamson mural. ▼

MULTI-FAMILY
THE RESIDENCE AT MARINA BAY
IRMO, SOUTH CAROLINA

The Arnold Companies purchased Lake Murray Marina in 2002 with the intent of developing a first class, mixed-use project unlike anything else on Lake Murray. Large, high-end rental units along with a new marina center complete with ship store, marina office, and restaurant were planned and would become one of the first developments in the U.S. on a major lake with rental units and all amenities on-site.

So impressive were the plans for the development that pre-leasing allowed the first residential building to fill even as reservations were being taken for other units that were still under construction. Today, the former marina has been transformed into Lake Murray's new lakefront lifestyle destination known as Marina Bay. The development, designed to satisfy the need for luxury living on the lake without having to deal with the burdens of owning a home, has done just that.

Kelvin E. Washington, Sr., the Chairman of the Richland County Council, weighed in on Arnold's performance on the project. "I want to express my support and appreciation for Arnold Companies' many contributions to the Midlands of South Carolina, including their development of such attractions as Marina Bay in Richland County," Washington noted. "Arnold Companies' accessibility, professionalism and attention to detail have helped establish great rapport with the community, making it a solid known commodity residents and visitors can count on to deliver top quality residential, shopping, dining and other projects."

Miriam S. Atira, the President and CEO of the Capital City/Lake Murray Country Regional Tourism District, echoed Washington's comments in a letter commending Arnold Family Corporation in 2013. "This region is very fortunate to have the Arnold Family Corporation and their expertise in our community," she stated.

THE PALMS ON MAIN
DOWNTOWN COLUMBIA,
SOUTH CAROLINA

The Arnold Companies transformed an historic hotel in downtown Columbia into one of the city's most sought after addresses. A unique blend of Art Deco sophistication with today's most modern amenities, The Palms features 53 luxury apartments as well as impressive entry foyer, concierge services, covered parking, tropical pool, lush garden-style landscaping, business center, restaurants, and retail space.

MIXED USE

Shining examples of Arnold's signature mixed-use developments include Vista Lofts and 700 Gervais Offices & Entertainment space, known as the Vista Station, both in Columbia. Home to numerous restaurants, professional offices, and multi-family apartment units, the 48,938 square foot Vista Lofts won the Historic Columbia Foundation's award for "New Construction in a Historic Context" in 2003.

▲ *The Palms on Main - Interior View.*

The Depot Building, home to Wet Willies and Jillian's. ▼

▲ *The Residence at Marina Bay - Resort Style Pool.*

RETAIL/ENTERTAINMENT

The Historic Columbia Foundation spotlighted Arnold Construction in 1999 for its renovation and expansion of the 1850-era train depot building. Part of the Vista Station complex, the Depot Building houses Wet Willie's and Jillian's, an entertainment restaurant with bars, game room, and outdoor patio seating.

MEDICAL OFFICES

Arnold Construction was awarded the construction and site development for 5,436 square foot Carolina Shoulder and Knee Medical Office. The company also completed the Parkside Center, which is home to medical offices, retail, and restaurants.

INDUSTRIAL

In 1998, Arnold Companies completed the Windhill Center, a 50,000 square foot industrial distribution site with warehouses, offices, and loading docks. Arnold also built the Farmer's Market Laboratory in Cayce, South Carolina. The 20,917 square foot facility was one of the first buildings built in conjunction with the public/private partnership at the Farmer's Market location.

RESTAURANTS

Examples of the Arnold Company's quality development and management projects in the food service arena are Liberty on the Lake, the new lakefront destination on Lake Murray at Marina Bay; Wild Wings Café, a 13,000 square foot restaurant and entertainment space; Tsunami, one of Columbia's top sushi restaurants located in Columbia's Vista Station complex; and Basil Thai Cuisine in Mount Pleasant, South Carolina.

A LEGACY OF SERVICE

Serving the people of the Midlands region for two decades, Ben Arnold and his team of professionals appreciate the importance of preserving South Carolina's natural resources for future generations. The company fully embraces green building techniques and uses energy-efficient appliances and fixtures in its projects.

In 2011, Arnold Construction won its fourth consecutive annual award from the South Carolina Chamber of Commerce as one of "South Carolina's Fastest Growing Companies." Upon accepting the award, Ben Arnold was quoted as saying, "We are honored to be invited and associated with South Carolina's Fastest Growing Companies. This is our fourth year in the Top 25, and every year we are impressed with the level of competitors and the diversity of

Marina Bay, Irmo, SC - Home to The Residence at Marina Bay, Lake Murray Marina, Liberty on the Lake, The Boat Club and The Peanut Man. ▼

Marina Bay's Marina Center, Liberty on the Lake restaurant, view from the docks. ▼

the participants. We are fortunate to operate in a state with such a bright future."

The companies operating under the Arnold family umbrella are poised to continue to remain a bright part of the region's future for years to come. Adhering to Ben Arnold's philosophy of "surround yourself with the right people, have a balanced life, read, and strive to learn as much as you can," Arnold Companies intend to continue striving for excellence and making their mark on the local landscape.

▲The Arnold Companies incorporates unique art into its developments adding excitement not found in traditional real estate developments. Some examples of this are the 40' x 25' mural on The Palms that faces Main Street and the bullet trains and box car mural on the Vista Station pictured above.

The Vista Lofts from the PNC Bank side view. ▼

Windhill Center - Industrial. ▲

Paul Mitchell - The School (located in the Depot Building). ▼

Photo by Paul Ringger

COLUMBIA

Owen Steel Company

Exceeding Expectations

Perhaps the greatest testament to the value of the Owen name in the structural steel industry is the fact that the original company name was retained by three subsequent owners of the business that was founded in 1936 by Franklyn D. Owen, Sr. Over the years, Columbia-based Owen Steel became one of the largest steel fabrication businesses in America.

Columbia seemed the logical choice for the location of Franklyn Owen's new business venture. Over the decades, steel fabrication evolved into a major industry in Columbia. In addition, the nature of Owen's work attracted some of the top professional talent in the industry to live in Columbia, where they enjoy the city's comfortable pace of life along with the excitement of working on the most complex and iconic projects on the skylines of the nation's largest cities. Columbia also provides many logistical advantages for steel fabrication, including interstate access, rail service and port access for ocean freight along with an airport offering direct flights to virtually every major city where the company today does business.

CORE VALUES AND A CLEAR MISSION

Owen Steel's position at the forefront of the structural steel industry is a result of its policy of investing in people, equipment, technology, and processes, and to consistently delivering high-quality results that exceed the expectations of its clients. That commitment has resulted in Owen Steel's reputation for quality and service throughout the structural steel industry, but especially in the highly competitive New York market. Over the past decade, the Columbia plant has been an integral part of rebuilding the World Trade Center site, fabricating the steel for the National September 11 Memorial and Museum, Tower 3, the West Side Highway infrastructure, and components of the PATH hub.

Owen has also fabricated steel for major projects from Boston to Florida to Chicago, to Chicago and through the Midwest, and even offshore to the Caribbean and South America. Owen Steel was also the choice for many other large and notable projects in New York, Philadelphia, New Jersey, Washington, Atlanta and South Florida, and of course, in the company's own back yard in Columbia.

Owen Steel typically provides employment for between 200 and 225 people in Columbia, with about 40 in the office. Owen Steel is represented on the boards of most of Columbia's major local business organizations, including the Chamber of Commerce and Midlands Technical College, and on many national industry boards.

"Every year, at our service awards luncheon, I am amazed at how many people are celebrating not just 20 and 30 years, but 40 and even 45 years with Owen Steel," states David Zalesne, the company's President. "It creates a unique sense of pride and family in the company, and gives our employees from all around the Columbia region a sense of stability, through the good and the bad economic times."

▼ *Steel fabricated at Owen in Columbia erected in one of the tallest buildings in Midtown Manhattan.*
—*Photo by C Thomas Kieren*

◀▼ *Inside the plant, fitters and welders assemble large steel components for Owen projects.*

▼ *Steel for University of South Carolina, Darla Moore School of Business.*

Photo by Paul Ringger

Heathwood Hall

Columbia's age three through grade 12 independent school where students learn to expect more.

As one of the oldest independent schools in Columbia, Heathwood Hall is located on a 122-acre campus just a quarter mile from the banks of the Congaree River. Its expansive campus serves as a perfect symbol of the in-depth, relationship-based, immersive learning Heathwood families have come to expect since the school was founded in 1951. "We know that what sets us apart is not only our academic expertise, but our collaborative approach that envelops each

student in active, joyful learning," says Dr. Michael Heath, Head of School. "We prepare ambitious, curious and interesting students not only to succeed in college, but to continually feel excited by life and the life of the mind."

Heathwood is an Episcopal school that takes seriously its tradition of respecting the dignity of every person. The school has been open to students of color from the very beginning and continues to celebrate diversity in its community today. Weekly chapel services are welcoming of all students, faculty and staff regardless of their religious beliefs. Students of all ages participate in service projects benefitting non-profits in the local community. Heathwood was the first school in the Midlands to include community service in its graduation requirements.

A STUDENT-CENTERED CULTURE

Over its more than sixty years of service, Heathwood has gained national acclaim with a college preparatory program built around the philosophy of knowing and teaching each child as an individual. Students at Heathwood are inspired by some of the most honored independent school faculty in South Carolina. These leaders challenge each student with much more than classroom lectures and memorized dates and facts. Analyzing information and collaborating with others in a group setting to solve difficult problems serve as the philosophical centerpiece for Heathwood's program of inspiring students to view learning as a lifelong experience and a path to personal excellence.

Unique programs and opportunities during and after the regular school day foster curiosity and expertise among students of all ages. Academic clubs and fine arts classes help nurture individual talents. Upper School students follow their interests across the globe for one week each year through Winterim, a week-long immersion in a particular area of study.

The PEAK outdoor leadership program offers ropes course experience, wilderness self-reliance, and leadership development, as well as canoeing and kayaking experience on campus and beyond. SEED, the environmental education program, inspires learning about conservation, scientific rigor, and self-reflection.

Heathwood Hall's twenty-five different athletics teams, award-winning arts programs, and a multitude of clubs give students countless opportunities to develop their interests and talents beyond academics.

What kind of school do you expect for your child? Come see what you can expect from a Heathwood education.

Suzanne Nagy, 5th grade English teacher, works with students on prepositions. ◄

Upper School students take a break between classes. ▼

Kindergarten students enjoy sharing their work with each other and with their teacher, Sandra Hall. ▼▼

WiSTV 10

Serving the Midlands For More Than Sixty Years

The 18-0 victory of the South Carolina Gamecocks over the North Carolina Tarheels on November 7, 1953 was more than a shutout in the long-held football rivalry between the two universities. The game that day also marked the inaugural broadcast for WIS television as the matchup was beamed live into the homes of football fans across the Midlands.

▲ The WIS News team in the 80's Ed Carter, Susan Audé, Joe Dagget, and Joe Pinner.

WIS evening news team (l to r: Sports Director Rick Henry, Chief Meteorologist John Farley, News Anchor Judi Gatson, Meteorologist Ben Tanner, News Anchor Dawndy Mercer-Plank). ▼

Over the next sixty-plus years, WIS evolved into its position today as the third-longest continuously operating television station in South Carolina. WIS continues to serve the Midlands region of South Carolina. Representing eleven counties, the station operates in the 77th television Designated Market Area ranked by Nielsen. WIS reaches over 400,000 television households in a viewing area that includes Richland, Lexington, Calhoun, Kershaw, Fairfield, Newberry, Saluda, Orangeburg, Clarendon, Sumter, and Lee Counties. The broadcast area's NBC affiliate, WIS remains one of the country's most dominant television stations, far-and-away the market news leader in the region for most of its history.

Growth and Service Over the Years

Originally owned by the Broadcasting Company of the South, WIS was the fourth television station to sign on in South Carolina. WIS Television would share the same three-letter call sign with its sibling radio station, Those call letters stood for "Wonderful Iodine State" in reference to the abundance of iodine in the soil of South Carolina. In 1932, G. Richard Shafto became General Manager of WIS Radio, helping make it one of the leading broadcast voices in the Southeast. He also played a huge role in forming WIS Television and broadcasting in South Carolina. Shafto helped launch the Broadcast and Communications Archives at the University of South Carolina's McKissick Museum. At the museum you will find his plaque as the first inductee to the South Carolina Broadcasters Hall of Fame.

Charles Batson signed WIS Television on the air and remained its president and general manager until his retirement three decades later.

WIS-TV was fortunate to gain the solitary VHF license in Columbia and serving the Midlands region, providing many people in that part of South Carolina with their first clear reception of a television signal. Channel 10 was one of only two stations that brought a clear signal to much of the outlying portions of the market until the arrival of cable television in the 1970s.

WIS-TV Channel 10 originally began broadcasting from a self-supporting tower atop its studios on Bull Street. In 1959, the station activated its transmitter tower in Lugoff. The tallest structure located east of the Mississippi River at the time, the new location more than doubled the station's coverage area and provided at least secondary coverage of all but five of the state's 46 counties. The station's original tower is still a longtime fixture of Columbia's skyline, especially during the holiday season when it is transformed into a "Christmas tree of lights."

The Broadcasting Company of the South acquired several other television stations over the years. It was renamed as Cosmos Broadcasting Corporation in 1965, with WIS radio and television serving as its flagship stations. Later in the decade, Liberty Life reorganized itself as The Liberty Corporation, with Liberty Life and Cosmos as subsidiaries. Cosmos sold WIS radio in 1986, but kept the WIS call letters for channel 10. Liberty sold off its insurance businesses in 2000, bringing channel 10 directly under the Liberty Corporation banner. On August 25, 2005, Liberty agreed to merge with Montgomery, Alabama-based Raycom Media. At the time, Raycom already owned another television station in the market and could not keep both stations because of FCC duopoly rules, so the company opted to keep WIS.

In 1991, after being known on-air as "WIS-TV 10" for most of its history, the station began branding itself as simply "WIS." The "-TV" suffix had been officially dropped from its call sign the year before. In 2003, the station re-branded as "WIS News 10" for both general and newscast branding purposes, and in 2012 adopted the "WIS Investigates" branding

▲ Joe Pinner aka Mr. Knozit has been a WIS favorite for over 50 years.

Investigative reporters Jack Kuenzie and PJ Randhawa on set. ▼

as it launched an investigative reporting focus.

The WIS office and studios are located at 1111 Bull Street in the heart of downtown Columbia. Construction of the television studio was completed in November 1949 when it was added to the original building that housed WIS radio. The iconic colonial brick building with white columns is a landmark in Columbia, and the original WIS Television signage remains on the Gervais Street side of the building. The rectangular wood-paneled lobby is one of the few areas of the interior that remains unchanged today. On November 4, 2010, WIS began broadcasting its local newscasts in high definition. With the upgrade, the news set received a facelift, a fresh graphics package was introduced, and the station changed its weather branding to "First Alert Weather." The WIS newsroom was remodeled in 2013 with state-of-the-art equipment to accommodate the digital workflow, operational and technological transformation of the station's newsgathering business.

Judi Gatson and Dawndy Mercer Plank during WIS News 10 at 5:00. ▼

A TRUSTED PUBLIC SERVANT TODAY

WIS has maintained its position of leadership in the market for more than sixty years. It has remained on the cutting edge of technology as new innovations have transformed the world of television since the first large wooden consoles housing small black-and-white screens first appeared in American households.

With 105 full-time and ten part-time employees, WIS continually strives to remain at the vanguard of top quality reporting and news dissemination. WIS newscasts are regularly ranked at the top in virtually all sectors of competition. The early adoption of new technology has helped to foster the company's ever-changing approach to timely content delivery to its readers and viewers.

In September 1963, WIS introduced one of the first seven o'clock PM newscasts in the country. The debut was timed to coincide with the expansion of NBC's iconic "Huntley-Brinkley Report" from fifteen to thirty minutes in length. The "7:00 Report" remains one of the station's premier newscasts.

In 1963, WIS introduced "Mr. Knozit", a children's program that garnered a Peabody Award for "distinguished achievement and meritorious public service." The program featured Joe Pinner who hosted the show until 2000 and, as "Papa Joe" Pinner, continues to make public appearances for WIS and hosts the weather portion of the Friday twelve noon newscast.

In 1970, WIS-TV premiered Awareness, a weekly public affairs program focusing on social and political issues concerning the African American population of the Midlands. This prestigious program celebrates its 44th anniversary on WIS in 2014.

A TECHNOLOGY LEADER IN THE 21ST CENTURY

In 1997, WIS embarked on an entirely new way of sharing information with the people of the Midlands, South Carolina, and beyond. WIStv.com was launched when few television stations at that time had websites. WIStv.com was the first website in the area to provide regular news updates. The website now registers more than seven million page views per month with over nine million page views on the WIS mobile app. There are over 100,000 "likes" on WIS Facebook and those numbers continue to grow exponentially.

The management and staff at WIS are deeply committed to the notion that reporting information in a timely and trustworthy manner on all platforms (TV, internet, social media) is the best way to continue to serve the community. The station's aggressive approach to breaking news, investigative reporting, and sharing the stories of those who are doing special things in the community is complimented online with expanded

WIS Production control allows for full high definition broadcasts of all WIS produced programming. ▼▼

storytelling, more data, and related stories and subject matter.

When smartphones began transforming the way we communicate, WIS and its parent company immediately worked to develop and implement free local news and weather apps to make sure the station's reporting and weather forecasting were present in the mobile space. As technology has matured, so have the offerings of WIS on all platforms. The station was the first in the Columbia area market to live stream all of its newscasts on its website. A few years later, WIS began offering live streaming of its newscasts and breaking news on its mobile apps.

As social media caught fire in the late 2000s, WIS was quick to adopt Facebook, Twitter, Google+, Instagram, and other channels to expand upon the station's commitment to the Midlands.

The awards that WIS has garnered are many, reflecting the hard work of the station's employees and the pride they take in serving the public:

- Winner of the South Carolina Broadcasters Association "Station of the Year" Award six times over the last ten years, most recently in 2014.

- Winner of the Richard M. Uray "Service Project of the Year" Award in 2012 for the station's "Families Helping Families" initiative.

- Multiple "Best of Columbia" Awards from Columbia Metropolitan Magazine.

- Multiple "Best of the Best" Awards from Free Times.

- South Carolina Associated Press "Best Website" Award in 2009 and 2010.

- Emmy Award for "Best Newscast" in the Southeast Region in 2003, 2005, and 2009.

Equally important to the station's staff and management is the fact that WIS has become a trusted member of the community, relied upon daily to keep viewers informed of events around the region, the nation, and the world. When there is a need, WIS dedicates all its resources to making a difference.

WIS volunteers regularly turn out to help thousands of children get gifts at Christmas with the Palmetto Project and Families Helping Families, now in its twenty-fourth year. They can also be found working on school supply and food drives, the American Red Cross annual blood drive, the Cultural Council's "Color the Arts" initiative, the McDaniels Golf Tournament, Operation Stars & Stripes Troop Supply Drive, the Women's Heart and Sole 5 Miler, and other civic and charitable efforts.

Serving the public has been the mission of WIS since the station first went on the air more than sixty years ago. Its commitment to the future is just as solid.

▲ The Christmas lights atop the WIS tower are a holiday tradition in Columbia.

The WIS Newsroom was redesigned and rebuilt in 2013 to include state of the art technology and digital workflow. ▼

Mungo Homes

Celebrating 60 years of our family building for your family!

Michael J. Mungo was a sheet rock installer working his way through multiple academic degrees at the University of South Carolina when he founded his own company in 1954 and pioneered land development as a viable profession. Over the past sixty years, Mungo Homes has been one of the largest residential developers in South Carolina, but also one of the nation's

leading home building operations. Mungo brought development and construction innovation to the Midlands by building the first neighborhood outside the municipality to have water and sewer, rolled concrete curbs and gutters, and uniform street lighting. He included amenities such as swimming pools and tennis courts in his neighborhoods. Mungo Homes was the first in the area to initiate restrictive covenants in its communities and set a standard for built-in garages in homes of all price ranges.

Mungo's sons, Stewart and Steven, both graduates of Wofford College, joined their father in home construction and land development and continue the family business today. With a third generation now involved in the day to day operation of the company, Mungo Homes has risen to the number thirty-seven spot among home builders nationwide as ranked by Builder magazine. Growth and expansion of the business outside South Carolina has led to Mungo Homes now putting their personal signature on new

homes in eight markets in North Carolina, Georgia, and Alabama.

A Reputation for Quality

Michael Mungo founded the business on the principles of quality, integrity, and value, and his sons continue that tradition today in each of the family of companies under the corporate umbrella.

As principals, Stewart and Steven remain heavily involved in the day to day operations of the business and, unlike national builders, are accessible to buyers and homeowners and are often seen in the model homes and neighborhoods. And because Mungo Homes is a family-owned business, their dedication is to the complete satisfaction of their homeowners, not to a board of directors. Their uncompromising focus is on satisfying a variety of tastes and lifestyles and building high-quality, award-winning homes.

When the housing market took a sharp downturn in 2007 and many national builders were rocked and shocked, Mungo Homes not only survived but thrived. Beginning with that downturn, Mungo expanded its operations and began building new homes in Raleigh, North

▲ Owners Steven Mungo and Stewart Mungo.

Carolina; Sumter, South Carolina; and Savannah, Georgia. Having the founder's sons at the helm on a daily basis with their accessibility to buyers and homeowners alike helped create an environment of stability as solid as the foundations of the homes they build.

Unparalleled building expertise has also played a major role in the company's continued success. Mungo's builders of new homes undergo continuing education to maintain their cutting edge skills. And they take great pride in their numerous initiatives on sustainability in their construction practices.

As good stewards of the environment, all Mungo homes are built with energy-saving features such as low-flow plumbing fixtures, Energy Star appliances, radiant barrier roof sheathing, and programmable thermostats, to name a few. In addition, each and every home is tested by an independent third party and given a HERS rating to ensure energy efficiency. These efforts ensure that each Mungo Home is on the cutting edge of efficiency, affordability, and convenience and is greener, healthier, and more cost-efficient to operate.

The company's commitment to excellence has been recognized by its industry peers on several occasions. In 2012, Builder magazine named Mungo Homes "America's Best Builder" for overall achievement in housing and excellence in finance/operations, design/construction, customer service/quality, community/industry service and marketing. That same year, the company was also recognized by the National Association of Home Builders for the innovative "hauSmart" program (an exclusive to Mungo Homes) that embraces the most progressive construction techniques to create homes that are healthier for residents and the environment and are more cost-efficient to operate. In addition, Mungo Homes is a recipient

of the National Housing Quality Award, one of the home building industry's highest recognitions for quality achievement and operational excellence, the only South Carolina-based builder ever to achieve that recognition.

Among the many lessons that Stewart and Steven Mungo learned from their father is that along with success comes responsibility. Both brothers recognize their role as community leaders and are honored to participate on many civic boards and philanthropic committees. In addition, the Mungo family believes in giving back to the very community that has been responsible for their success by supporting organizations such as the National Kidney Foundation, Harvest Hope Food Bank, the Columbia Free Medical Clinic, Pawmetto Lifeline Animal Shelter, EdVenture Children's Museum, Oliver Gospel Mission, and Families Helping Families to name only a few.

Echerer Painting
Excellence at Work

*S*ince its founding in 1959, Echerer Painting has had a multi-fold mission that has guided the direction of the company throughout its existence. "Our goal has been to expand our appeal while at the same time increasing our business," states Lorenz Echerer, the founder of Echerer Painting. "We also continuously strive to enhance our reputation of being the contractor

of choice in the Southeast for coatings, wallcovering, and special finishes."

While the roots of the business that Echerer founded were in New York City, he moved the operation to Columbia in 1972 at the request of the many clients he had from the Palmetto State for whom he was working in Manhattan. Happy to accommodate those requests, he relocated to his present 6,000 square foot headquarters on Broad River Road in Columbia. Echerer's son, Larry, assumed the leadership of the business in 2005 and became the second generation

of the family to continue serving Echerer's many satisfied clients. Learning the business from the ground up had convinced the younger Echerer that following in his father's footsteps was the career he wanted to pursue. Continuing to enjoy the numerous business relationships he was instrumental in forging over the years, Lorenz Echerer remains a familiar fixture in the office every day.

EXCELLENCE IN EVERY JOB

The focus of every Echerer team member on every job is simple and singular – the

customer. The company's tagline of "Excellence at Work" is much more than just that. It defines Echerer's corporate culture and sharpens the focus of each company employee on infusing quality and excellence on each project on which Echerer has put its signature. Some of most recognized names who have turned to Echerer for their painting needs include Boeing, Nephron Pharmaceuticals, Palmetto Health Hospitals, Providence Hospitals, Lexington Medical Center, Jim Hudson Dealerships, and numerous churches. While most of their projects have been primarily in the

Installing some of the 7,000 gallons of paint needed to make Nephron Pharmaceutical a work of art. ▼

Columbia area, the company has also completed jobs for Columbia-based businesses that have work outside the state.

"Echerer is the last step in completing our clients' dreams of their beautiful new buildings or the upfit of existing buildings," Larry Echerer notes. "We are there to see the smiles on their faces when the job is complete. That is our ultimate goal – to make our clients happy!"

Their commitment to achieving that goal has resulted in Echerer Painting being ranked the largest commercial painting contractor in South Carolina and in the top 200 in the United States. That enviable ranking has translated not only into a long list of satisfied clients, but also into successful careers for the company's employees and their families in Columbia.

Those employees take very seriously their obligation to helping Echerer Painting fulfill its obligation to being a good corporate citizen. They take leadership roles in supporting local civic and charitable organizations, including Carolina Sunshine for Children, United Way of the Midlands, USC Educational Foundation, National Kidney Foundation and Friends of Richland County Library.

CEO and President, Larry Echerer. ▶

Turnover day at Palmetto Health. Every Echerer Team leader is here to make sure Excellence is turned over to the Hospital. ▼

NBSC, a division of Synovus Bank

Welcome Home to Community Banking

February 17, 1905 became a landmark date in the history of southern commerce. It was on that date in the historic farming town of Sumter, forty miles from South Carolina's capital city, that a visionary young man named C.G. Rowland quit his job with the local railroad and opened a new bank. The National Bank of South Carolina had taken

the first step on what would prove to be a truly amazing journey.

Originally operating his new bank out of a local grocery store, Rowland moved just two years later into more permanent offices. He proved to be a trusty steward of

underlying financial strength, its loyalty and dedication to its customers, and to the experience and business acumen of its bankers.

Throughout the 20th Century, NBSC developed a reputation for unsurpassed customer service while

Synovus Financial Corp., and a Columbus, Georgia-based financial services company with approximately $27 billion in assets. The 28 locally-branded divisions of Synovus Bank are located in some of the best markets in the Southeast with branches and ATMs in Georgia, Alabama, South Carolina, Florida, and Tennessee.

A REGIONAL NETWORK WITH A FOCUS ON COMMUNITY

As a member of the Synovus family, NBSC offers its customers the benefits of one of the strongest and most capable regional banking networks in the Southeast while maintaining its focus on community. This relationship-based delivery model sets NBSC apart from other financial institutions and creates a unique banking experience for the customer.

In addition to providing the banking services required by individual customers, NBSC has long been known for the complete range of financial products and services it offers to area businesses. That commitment began more than a century ago when the newly established bank helped local people launch some of the earliest businesses in the Midlands.

Over its more than a century of service, NBSC has proven to be a perfect fit for small and middle market businesses. Advanced technology and skilled professionals provide for great banking relationships. NBSC bankers understand that business customers want to know their banker and the banking team that supports their business. The ultimate goal of every NBSC banker is to provide unsurpassed customer service to each and every individual and business

▲ Midlands Leadership Team (l to r) standing: John "Fitz" King, Marcus Crosswell, Jennifer Blackhurst, Jessie Ford, Bill LaMotte, John Griggs (l to r) seated: Sam Baxter, Boyd Jones.

other people's money and a paragon of personal integrity. Rowland was probably unaware at the time that he was establishing the foundation of a value system that future NBSC bankers would continue to embrace for generations.

During the bleak years of the Great Depression, most of the nation's banks failed along with thousands of other businesses. Of the seven banks operating in Sumter during the 1930s, only NBSC weathered the Great Depression. Its survival was due to the bank's

practicing sound financial management. Assets grew steadily and branch offices were opened around the state, originally in the neighboring communities and later in major metropolitan areas. When NBSC moved into the Columbia market in 1965, it became the first new bank to open in the city in three decades.

In 1995, NBSC became part of Synovus Financial Corp. It operates today as a division of Synovus Bank, Member FDIC, a wholly-owned subsidiary of

account customer. The 21 national and regional awards for customer service that Synovus received in 2013 from Greenwich National Service Excellence Awards indicate NBSC bankers are achieving their goal.

In addition, NBSC is justifiably proud of the commitment it has made to its team members. For three consecutive years beginning in 2011, NBSC has been named to the list of "Best Places to Work in South Carolina" by SC Biz News, the South Carolina Chamber of Commerce and Best Companies Group.

Those team members understand the importance of being good corporate citizens. They are personally committed to helping improve the quality of life in the communities across the state in which NBSC maintains branch offices. From raising money for organizations such as the American Heart Association and March of Dimes to collecting food items for local food banks or clothing items for those less fortunate, NBSC associates are always giving back to their communities.

A COMMITMENT TO THE FUTURE

NBSC is strongly committed to the future of South Carolina, serving three major regions: Central, Upstate and Coastal. The bank's ambitious plans for growth in the state focus on building relationships.

"Our strength is catering to both the individual customer as well as to businesses," stated NBSC President and CEO Chuck Garnett. "In addition, the large corporate banking team within Synovus allows NBSC to serve the largest companies doing business in the state. We think South Carolina has a lot of positive momentum. There have been many significant economic development announcements in recent years. This business is going through a tremendous amount of change today and we foresee great opportunities ahead."

Banking products are provided by Synovus Bank, Member FDIC and Equal Housing Lender. Divisions of Synovus Bank operate under multiple trade names across the Southeast.

NBSC Main Office ▼

City of rivers, vistas, and dreams

C O L U M B I A

Columbia Urban League, Inc.

Empowering African-Americans and Others to Enter the Economic and Societal Mainstream

Chartered on April 13, 1967, the Columbia Urban League, an affiliate of the National Urban League that was founded in 1910, is a community-based, non-profit, non-partisan and inter-racial organization. The mission of the Columbia Urban League is to enable African-Americans and others to secure economic self-reliance, parity, power, and civil rights. The League implements its mission through evidenced-based intervention strategies as well as advocacy and dialogue in promoting common ground among community stakeholders in addressing community challenges and opportunities. The League focuses on empowering the less fortunate and underserved in becoming productive members of society. The staff views themselves as positive change agents for uplifting those in need.

PROGRAMS TO EMPOWER PEOPLE

The Columbia Urban League employs several signature initiatives under its youth leadership development component:

- Equal Opportunity Day Dinner and Annual Fund Campaign highlights the importance of equal opportunity in empowering communities and changing lives. It also provides resources enabling the Columbia Urban League to fulfill its mission of serving those in need.

- Facilitation of fair housing education and outreach activities in Lexington County by educating the community on their rights under Title VIII of the Fair Housing Act, including assistance to community members with filing complaints when subjected to impediments in housing.

- Supplemental Nutrition Assistance Program (SNAP) is designed to assist unemployed SNAP recipients in obtaining suitable employment.

- Summer Work Experience Leadership Program (SWELP) introduces teens to work ethics and to work experience.

- Youth Leadership Development Institute (YLDI) prepares and assists youth, in foster care, with transitioning to independent living.

- Youth Development Academy (YDA) exposes youth, ages 10-13, to a developing culture of high expectations and confidence.

- Project Ready Mentor prepares disadvantaged and underserved youth for post-secondary education, the workforce, and the challenges and opportunities of life.

- College Internship Program (CIP) is designed to reduce the brain drain by connecting college students with internships during their college career.

Additionally, other signature programs include: Science, Technology, Engineering and Mathematics (STEM) Youth Expo; I AM Woman Health and Wellness program designed to reduce obesity and influence the health and wellness of women two generations at a time; Civility promotes a quality of life (QOL) measurement that teaches us how to connect successfully with others and how to live together with mutual respect.

"At the heart of the Columbia Urban League is compassion manifested in social activity," stated Frank Mood, Jr., retired senior partner with Haynsworth Sinkler Boyd, PA and Columbia Urban League board member. "The activity may be providing educational tools for our children, career opportunities for our young people, necessities for those in need, or justice for those wronged. The League has no ulterior motive. Its purpose is the well-being of the community. An organization so committed inevitably enhances the spirit and enriches the lives of its people."

▲ Annual Fund Campaign & Equal Opportunity Day Dinner, pictured are, left to right, Mr. Ron Tryon, Ms. Charlene H. Keys, Dr. Marshall "Sonny" White, and Mr. James T. McLawhorn, Jr.

◄▼ Columbia Urban League Encourages Youth through its Annual STEM (Science, Technology, Engineering & Mathematics) program.

▼ Columbia Urban League Supplemental Nutrition Assistance Program (SNAP) employment initiative.

Buford Goff & Associates, Inc.
Built on Integrity

Technology runs our world today, but in the late 1960s, its application and advantages for business, industry, and government were just being discovered and coming into vogue. It was his passion for exploring the capabilities of the burgeoning new science that led H. Buford Goff, Jr. to leave his position as a member of the technical staff at Bell Telephone Laboratories and Vice-President of Marketing at Computer Labs, Inc. Goff's dream was to venture out on his own and establish a consulting engineering firm that would be built around cutting edge for utilities in the rapidly growing field of electric load control and management. Later, he expanded the firm's capabilities to support mechanical and electrical engineering services. This expansion provided a balance of traditional and highly technical disciplines to the company's professionals undertake. For over forty years the company has been providing innovative solutions to its clients by assembling a team of professionals and support personnel that are highly respected in markets in which the firm practices. Those

▲ BGA Officers & Directors with founder H. Buford Goff, Jr. (from left to right) Brian C. Melson, Keith E. Summer, H. Buford Goff, Jr., Dan E. Reider, and Michael E. Corbett.

▲ H. Buford Goff, Jr.—
Founder of BGA
Communications Tower ▲

SC State House Dome Lighting—
Columbia, SC ▼

technology, developing solid business relationships, and applying a strong work ethic.

Goff founded Buford Goff & Associates, Inc. (BGA) in Columbia in 1969 offering professional services that were initially focused on designing and implementing communications systems

support the complex engineering environments that are demanded on BGA's projects.

Always a forward thinker, Goff envisioned building on the technology that the Department of Defense was using and applying it to criminal justice facilities. In the mid 1970's, the South Carolina Department of Corrections awarded BGA the contract to design and implement an electronic perimeter system for the first new prison to be built by the State in decades. BGA capitalized on the "justice revolution" that characterized the 1970s, and soon began designing perimeter and security control systems for correctional facilities as far away as California. All of this activity occurred in parallel as the firm expanded into the field of supporting communications systems for state and local government entities.

markets include clients in the fields of healthcare, education, public safety, energy, homeland security, and criminal justice. BGA consistently provides the right balance of skills, experience and effort that have led to the successful completion of many communications network, school, healthcare facility, and detention projects.

Today, BGA has four unique, but interdependent engineering divisions:

- Mechanical
- Electrical
- Security Electronics
- Communications

All divisions share common offices and administrative support at the Columbia, South Carolina headquarters. The company employs a staff of thirty-five which includes registered engineers, IT specialists, business analysts, technical designers, and administrative personnel. BGA maintains professional registration in more than

BUFORD GOFF & ASSOCIATES TODAY

Improving the quality of life is at the forefront of every project

thirty states and is a member of the National Council of Engineering Examiners and the National Society of Professional Engineers.

In addition to its own employees, BGA maintains professional relationships with other firms in the areas of architectural, civil engineering, structural engineering, soils engineering, and communications law. These relationships significantly enhance the firm's capability to provide total engineering services.

MECHANICAL AND ELECTRICAL GROUPS

The Mechanical and Electrical Groups provide engineering services for a wide variety of projects that encompass healthcare, correctional, institutional, high-rise commercial buildings, public safety, energy, and educational facilities. Over thirty percent of the firm's projects are renovations projects. Additionally, these departments provide specialized services that include analytical engineering, studies, utility master plans, and systems troubleshooting.

BGA professionals in the Mechanical Group understand the importance of designing systems that meet each client's unique requirements. Each mechanical system design is performed within the client's budget and staffing constraints with primary emphasis on functionality, life-cycle costs, and maintainability.

The experienced staff in the Electrical Group focus on the design of power systems, lighting systems, power generation systems, transient protection, backup power systems, power conditioning, and specialized electrical/electronic systems employing the latest technology available.

SECURITY GROUP

The engineers in BGA's Security Electronics Group are recognized on a national basis for their understanding of the unique requirements of correctional and justice facilities, technical knowledge of systems, and the successful implementation of integrated security systems for these facilities.

Security engineering is performed on a national basis. The firm has provided professional services for correctional and detention facilities located throughout the United States ranging in cost from $2 million to over $500 million. Security electronics communications systems for more than 500 projects totaling over $35 billion in construction have been designed by BGA.

COMMUNICATIONS GROUP

Communications and information technology systems are critical to the operations of any agency or enterprise. As an example, reliable and available communities systems that support law enforcement, fire and emergency medical services, and critical infrastructure industries are required under all conditions and all times. The Communications Group at BGA specializes in the implementation and integration of these complex systems as evidenced by the successful planning, design and deployments of numerous systems for utilities and government entities.

BGA specializes in the implementation and integration of complex communications and information technology systems. Specific areas of expertise include public safety, homeland security, criminal justice, and utility market segments. BGA continues to provide professional services on major networks throughout the United States and abroad including

▲ Jim Hudson Lexus – Columbia, SC
PHOTO BY JHS ARCHITECTS

regional, statewide, and multistate programs.

"We are proud and thankful that BGA has been entrusted by our clients to provide engineering services on significant projects within our home state of South Carolina and throughout the United States," Goff stated recently. "The repeated selection of BGA by our clients reflects the successful teaming relationships fundamental to successful projects. BGA is committed to supporting the ever-changing and demanding technological challenges as has been demonstrated by the historical performance of BGA. We look forward to the opportunities to continue to serve our existing clients."

Palmetto Health Baptist Parkridge – Columbia, SC ▼

Photo by Paul Ringger

Callison Tighe & Robinson, LLC

Six decades of service to our clients and our community

With roots dating to 1947 that run deep in the local and state communities, Callison Tighe & Robinson, LLC is a firm not just of committed attorneys, but also of people who contribute to the Midlands of South Carolina and the legal profession.

▲ Managing Member Mike Tighe stands in front of a complete set of weapons made at the Palmetto Armory and Iron Works in 1851.
—Photo by Rick Smoak.

▼▼ The firm's offices were built on the site of the Palmetto Iron Works and Armory.
—Photos by Rick Smoak.

It began when Preston Callison formed a real estate law practice in Columbia. Michael W. Tighe, then an assistant South Carolina attorney general, left the employ of the state and joined Mr. Callison in 1971, expanding the firm's practice to include title insurance defense. The firm took on its current name in 1983, when Ralph C. "Robbie" Robinson merged his practice into the firm.

The firm has grown to its present size of more than 20 attorneys with diverse practices, among them commercial real estate, litigation, workers' compensation, employment law, environmental, government and business law. The firm regularly represents clients across a wide range of industries, including insurance, banking, development, construction, education, health care and manufacturing.

The firm also remains true to Mr. Callison's original commitment to treating clients as individuals. The attorneys at Callison Tighe strive to understand each client's distinct situation in recommending a cost-efficient, customized strategy as unique as the client's needs and challenges demand.

The firm's attorneys are licensed in all trial and appellate courts in South Carolina and the federal system, with several of their number admitted to practice before the United States Supreme Court. The firm's litigators have handled a variety of cases for individuals, local businesses and national concerns. Its business and transactional lawyers represent clients in complex commercial development and financing matters.

As the firm has grown, so has its reputation. Callison Tighe has been recognized in *The Best Law Firms in America*, and several of its attorneys have been listed in the companion publication, *The Best Lawyers in America*. Members have been recognized as *Super Lawyers* and listed among the *Legal Elite of the Midlands* as well.

The firm's attorneys have heeded the call to lead local, state and national legal organizations. Member D. Reece Williams III recently served as president of the American Board of Trial Advocates. He and member Ian McVey have served as president of the Richland County Bar.

The firm is also active in civic organizations in the Midlands. Its members work with numerous charitable and non-profit organizations, including Welvista, Inc., The University of South Carolina Ex Libris Society, SC Equality, the South Carolina Victims Assistance Network, the Junior League of Columbia and Civitans.

The firm and its attorneys enjoy giving back to the community, making substantial donations to worthy local causes such as Harvest Hope Food Bank, the Oliver Gospel Mission, the National Kidney Foundation, the South Carolina Philharmonic, and the Cultural Council of Richland and Lexington Counties.

Riverbanks Zoo and Garden

Education. Conservation. Exploration.

A journey across several continents would be necessary for anyone wishing to view tigers, sharks, baboons, giraffes, and zebras, but each of those animals in addition to the more than 350 other species of wild creatures are viewed by more than one million visitors annually at Columbia's Riverbanks Zoo and Garden. Since the site opened in April 1974, the 170-acre facility has evolved into one of the Palmetto State's premier attractions and has been acclaimed as one of the finest zoos and most beautiful gardens in the United States.

"The goal here four decades ago was to create and sustain a world-class zoo," explains Susan O'Cain, the zoo's Communications and Public Relations Specialist. "The focus at that time, and what we strive for today, is educating the public on the conservation and care of some of our world's most amazing wildlife.

Our staff delights in educating our many visitors on the worldwide conservation efforts of our many endangered species and the unique challenges in caring for exotic animals."

Upwards of 2,000 mammals, reptiles, amphibians, and birds can be viewed in the various habitat exhibits across the 100 acres of the zoo's portion of the site. Animal caretakers conduct special demonstrations relating to various species housed and cared for at the facility:

- Gorillas
- Kangaroos
- Elephants
- Snakes
- Aquatic life
- Penguins (twice daily feedings)

Hands-on interactive activities also ensure that all ages find something exciting at Riverbanks. A trackless children's train winds through the wooded site. Visitors can learn the proper techniques for scaling heights on the rock-climbing wall. A new zip line and vertical ropes challenge course also adds to the excitement. Pony rides are available for younger children, and visitors of all ages enjoy feeding the zoo's giraffes and exotic birds.

Educational activities abound at Riverbanks Zoo and Garden. Children are welcomed at the zoo's day camp and at supervised overnight sessions where they gain a better understanding of the various species with which we share our planet. Family programs offer age-specific activities. Visitors can also pre-register for the zoo's many behind-the-scenes Adventure Tours.

An award-winning tourist attraction in the heart of South Carolina, Riverbanks has earned a national reputation as one of America's best zoos and the perfect place to connect with and learn

▲ A young zoo guest feeds the sociable lorikeets.
—Photo by Robin Vondrak Photography

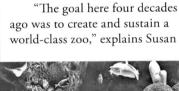

▼ Guests can watch daily fish feedings at Riverbanks' Aquarium-Reptile Complex.
—Photo by Richard W. Rokes

▲ Riverbanks Botanical Garden is considered one of the nation's most beautiful and inspiring public gardens. —Photo by Andy Cabe

about the world's wildlife and wild places. In fact, the zoo is a two-time winner of the Governor's Cup award for South Carolina's Most Outstanding Tourist Attraction from the South Carolina Chamber of Commerce. Other accolades include "Best Local Attraction" by readers of The State Newspaper, "Favorite Day Trip" by readers of Charlotte Parent Magazine, and "Top Field Trip Attraction" by Carolina Field Trips Magazine.

The garden also is considered the perfect venue for hosting private events. The Magnolia Room is often reserved for weddings and private receptions.

Leading the zoo's full-time staff and volunteers is one of the longest serving zoo directors in the nation. Satch Krantz began his career in 1973 and became Riverbanks Zoo's executive director in 1976. He is one

Garden annually—a remarkable feat given that tourism in general is concentrated along the state's coast in places like Charleston and Myrtle Beach. In addition, approximately forty percent of the Zoo's annual attendance is comprised of visitors who live fifty miles or more outside of Columbia. The Zoo's appeal to this vast number of people makes Riverbanks a powerful economic driver in the Midlands. Studies

▲ A koala, one of the zoo's most beloved animals. Riverbanks' koalas were acquired through a sister-state relationship between South Carolina and Queensland, Australia.
—Photo by Richard W. Rokes

▲ —Photo by Richard W. Rokes

▲ A male western lowland gorilla at Riverbanks pictured in the lush Ndoki Forest habitat. —Photo by Richard W. Rokes.

A GARDEN OF DELIGHTS

The other attraction at the site, the 70-acre botanical garden, has also received a long list of impressive kudos. The garden was hailed by Horticulture magazine as one of the nations' ten gardens that inspire and was named one of twenty great botanical gardens and arboretums across North America by HGTV®.

Nestled along the scenic lower Saluda River, Riverbanks Botanical Garden boasts beautiful natural woodlands, themed gardens, historic ruins and more than 4,300 species of native and e/xotic plants. The garden is listed on the National Register of Historic Places for the numerous historic landmarks dating to the early 1800s and to the American Civil War.

of only three American zoo directors that have served as president of both the Association of Zoos and Aquariums and the World Association of Zoos and Aquariums.

Krantz earned his reputation from active, hands-on experience at the zoo and inspirations found in the world's wild places. He has taken more than a dozen safaris to six different African countries and has walked 120 miles across Tsavo National Park in Kenya.

"Riverbanks is without question one of Columbia's most unique and valuable assets," Krantz states. "As South Carolina's largest gated tourist attraction, Riverbanks also is one of the nation's premier zoological parks and botanical gardens. More than one million people visit the Zoo and

have shown that the Zoo pumps more than $60 million into the local economy each year and creates more than 700 jobs in the area."

▼ A young zoo guest admires flamingos.
—Photo by Robin Vondrak Photography

Tyler Construction Group

Simple Philosophies That Work

Walter S. and Elaine Tyler founded Tyler Construction in Columbia in December 1979 with a clear vision: to build commercial, military, and industrial projects with the complete satisfaction of each of the company's clients as their top priority. Tyler understood that success in the construction business was much like that of a baseball pitcher.

"In construction, you are remembered by your last job," Tyler quips. "Just like in baseball, a pitcher is remembered for his last outing."

Tyler felt that there was much to be said for the simple things in life, including operating his business on the simple, yet intrinsic philosophies that would be the pillars of his company's success. "Hire motivated people," Tyler notes, "and keep them happy."

Adherence to these simple guidelines has been the cornerstone of Tyler Construction's success over the years and remains the principles on which the company

Spring Valley High School Stadium Upgrades; Richland County.

Saint Peter's Catholic Church Sanctuary Renovations; Columbia, SC.

operates today. Completing projects on time and within budget while maintaining a high quality of performance remain uppermost in the minds of each Tyler team member. The steady increase in the company's yearly volume of business since 1979 is due largely in part to the relationship that Tyler Construction has had and is pledged to maintain with the owners and architects. Even with the recent recession, the company's current volume of business is approximately $30 million annually and the outlook for the future is very bright.

A NEW BRAND FOR A FAMILIAR NAME

In 2007, Walter Tyler decided to pass the company he founded on to his two sons, Greg and Charles. He discovered that it was easier to start a new corporation than to sell the existing business to them. Tyler Construction Group was incorporated that year, and, while the founder remains involved in the business today, Charles is currently serving as the company's president. A 23-year veteran of the construction industry, Charles is joined in the ownership and operation of the business by his brother Greg.

The duo has religiously followed the founder's tenets in operating the business. Tyler Construction

Group relies on subcontractors for most of its trades, making management of this aspect of each project "essential" for success. Pursuant to this reliance, they contract the most highly qualified and competent sub-contractors and suppliers, and ensure they are treated fairly and are paid on time.

Tyler Construction also employs the right personnel for each project the company undertakes. Each of Tyler's superintendents has extensive knowledge and working experience for both new construction and renovation work. Along with office project management, the supervision on the jobsite is critical in maintaining a successful project.

Tyler Construction has remained a leader in its field due to the company's excellent reputation with sub-contractors, suppliers, architects, and owners and its willingness to work successfully with all parties on difficult projects, such as extensive renovations. Tyler professionals take great pride in being able to work through any issues that may arise during construction. They never present a problem to an owner or architect without also presenting a workable solution.

The management team at Tyler Construction Group focuses on in-depth, continuous training for their 50 in-house employees. The company takes advantage of its membership with Associated General Contractors (AGC) and participates in its OSHA training classes. Each Tyler superintendent has completed a 30-hour training course.

Tyler Construction Group's focus in recent years has been on serving the commercial and government sectors. The company has developed a unique niche: hardwood work for both public and

private projects. Tyler also offers pre-construction, budget estimates, scheduling, and a balanced combination of restoration as well as new construction services. The company's management team prides itself in working successfully with many state agencies, school districts, South Carolina National Guard, and Ft. Jackson Army Base. Tyler is currently working for the US Army Corps of Engineers in six states. Completing many federal projects for USACE has helped to keep Tyler Construction in good standing.

AN IMPRINT ON THE SKYLINE

Tyler Construction Group has added significantly to the skyline of the Midlands with the successful completion of numerous projects for a wide range of clients.

Developments in the education sector range from a restoration and addition project at Dent Middle School and a football stadium for Blythewood High School to a chiller plant for the University of South Carolina. Government projects include McKeller's Lodge at Fort Bragg, the Army Reserve Center at Fort Jackson, and additions and renovations to the City of Columbia Police Headquarters. From sanctuary renovations and a new Parish Life Center for St. Peter's Catholic Church to interior renovations for Our Lady of Perpetual Help Catholic Church in Camden, SC. From the Marble Slab Creamery in Columbia to the Graduate School at CIU. Tyler is the name that clients continue to trust for quality in all phases of the construction process from

pre-construction planning to final completion.

Those and numerous other successful projects have resulted in Tyler being recognized with several prestigious awards, including:

- Commendation of Excellence from the South Carolina Chamber of Commerce
- Safety Gold Award from Johnson Controls
- CEFPI 2008 Best in Class Award for additions and restoration work
- Recognition by The Historic Columbia Foundation for excellence in preservation and restoration work

"We are very optimistic about the future," Charles Tyler states, "and plan to continue the steady growth that has identified us over the years."

Dent Middle School; Forest Acres, SC.

◄▲ New 81st Army 81st Regional Support Command Headquarters; Ft. Jackson, SC.

◄▼ New Transient Student Barracks, Ft. Bragg, NC.

New Children's Garden Riverbanks Zoo; Columbia, SC. ▼

Jim Hudson Automotive Group

Honesty. Integrity. Customer Satisfaction.

Jim Hudson joined a very select group of South Carolinians when Governor Nikki Haley presented him with the "Order of the Palmetto Award" in 2013. "This award is in recognition of his extraordinary work and dedication to the citizens of our state," noted Governor Haley in the award ceremony. First presented in 1971, the award is considered to be the state's

highest civilian honor and recognizes a person's lifetime achievements and contributions to the State of South Carolina. Former recipients include governors, entertainers, noted authors, and philanthropists.

automobiles to the people of his adopted state and returning something to the communities that helped him reach his goal.

A native of Turkey, North Carolina, Hudson grew up on a tobacco farm. His grandfather, a strawberry farmer, convinced Jim to leave his rural setting and set his sights on a career in business. He moved to Columbia in 1961 where he worked as a part-time automobile salesman while he pursued a career as a licensed optician. Realizing that his true love was the automobile business, Hudson shelved his optician's license and devoted himself to becoming an automobile dealer.

"Becoming an Oldsmobile dealer became my life's ambition," Hudson recalls. "I love automobiles. I've always been fascinated by cars. The only time I ever got in trouble at school was one time when I went to look at some cars. And when I first began working at an auto dealership, I discovered I love working with people."

Working his way up through the ranks into a sales manager

▲ The Jim Hudson Management Company Group (left to right): Jack Parker, Vice President, Jim Hudson Automotive Group; Karyn Heimes, Director of Corporate Accounts; Jim Hudson, Owner; Keith Hudson, Owner; Don Deese, CPA, CFE, CGMA Jim Hudson Automotive Group; and Pete Olmstead, Parts & Service Director.

The award capped Hudson's half-century pursuit of his lifelong dream of providing quality

Jim Hudson Lexus, Killian Road, Columbia. ▼

Jim Hudson Cadillac, Killian Road, Columbia. ▼

position and eventually a partner in a Columbia dealership, Hudson continued to focus on someday seeing his name on a sign over his own business. In 1980, when Oldsmobile was ready to add a franchise in Columbia, Hudson was positioned to win the coveted dealership.

Hudson's dedication to customer satisfaction and his reputation for honesty and integrity led to rapid growth and expansion of his business. He soon added a second dealership, this one specializing in sports cars, including Maserati, Alfa Romeo, and Saab. A third location featuring Oldsmobile, GMC, Sterling, Suzuki, and Mitsubishi autos soon followed.

THREE DECADES OF GROWTH

That single Oldsmobile franchise in 1980 has evolved into a portfolio of automotive dealerships known today as Jim Hudson Automotive Group. The business includes six locations in South Carolina and Georgia:

- 3 in Columbia
- 1 in Lexington, South Carolina
- 1 in Irmo, South Carolina
- 1 in Augusta, Georgia

The various Jim Hudson Automotive Group locations now feature some of the premier names in the automotive industry:

- Buick
- Cadillac
- Ford
- GMC
- Hyundai
- Lexus
- Toyota
- Scion
- Saab

Shoppers in the market for new or pre-owned vehicles can scan Hudson's website www.jim-hudson.com for the most convenient location where they can find just the right vehicle to fit their individual needs and budget. Regardless of which Jim Hudson Automotive Group location they choose, customers can be assured of finding the same courtesy and professionalism from the sales staff. They will also find the best trained technicians in each dealership's service department alongside a parts department stocked with factory authorized parts and accessories.

A shining example of the "World Class" level of care that identifies Hudson's dealerships is the unique experience unveiled

▲ *Jim Hudson Hyundai, Greystone Blvd., Columbia.*

at Hudson's Hyundai franchise in Columbia. In order to give customers the red carpet treatment they deserve, Jim Hudson Hyundai created a New Owners Clinic as a night of information, food and fun. Every new Hyundai customer is invited to the Clinic within three months of their purchase to ask questions and learn more about their vehicle to ensure they are getting the most out of it. The parts manager, service technicians, and advisors are on hand to answer questions and make appointments as needed. The Clinic includes free oil changes for life, door prizes, and even cash during a Jim Hudson-themed trivia game. A catered three-course meal is served. The program, which draws

Jim Hudson Ford, Highway 378, Lexington, SC. ▼

Jim Hudson Toyota, Broad River Road, Irmo, SC. ▼

approximately eighty new owners and their guests each quarter, is a way to say "Thank you" to the local community for choosing Jim Hudson Automotive Group and making the dealership the number one volume Hyundai dealer in South Carolina.

That dedication to customer satisfaction has been the cornerstone of Jim Hudson Automotive Group's success over the years and has led to numerous industry awards. Beginning in 2001 and running for ten consecutive years, Hudson's Columbia Lexus dealership ranked number one or two in the nation for customer satisfaction. In 2002 and 2003, the Columbia dealership's second place ranking was only because Hudson's Augusta Lexus store moved up to the number one spot. Hudson's consistently high customer service rating was a major factor in Toyota's selection process when it came time to award another dealership in Columbia.

In addition, Hudson is understandably proud of other accolades his dealerships have received, including the "President's Award" from Toyota, and Cadillac Buick GMC's highest

award for excellence. Jim Hudson Automotive Group has been named the "Number One New Car Dealer in South Carolina" as well as having been featured three times in Time Magazine, including their Time Magazine Quality Dealer of the Year. In addition to being inducted into the Automotive Hall of Fame, Jim Hudson Automotive has been named Motor Trend Quality Dealer of the Year. And the entire Jim Hudson Automotive Group team takes great pride in the contribution that each team member has made to the company's recognition by Automotive News as one of the top 125 dealership groups in the U.S. The most recent honor was the selection by Lexus of Jim Hudson as the vice chairman of the National Dealerships Council for 2014.

THREE DECADES OF SERVICE TO THE COMMUNITY

Jim Hudson has always felt that along with success comes an obligation to serving the communities in which he and the members of his team live and work. From their sponsorship of The Columbia Art Center to being among the largest contributor's to

the Harvest of Hope food drive, Hudson's employees give of their own time and talents to help the less fortunate. Volunteer service also includes assisting other worthy civic and charitable organizations, including the Columbia East Rotary Club's Camp Okay, the Tree of Life Jewish Cultural Festival, the Ray Tanner Foundation, and the Autism Academy of South Carolina to name a few.

A firm believer in leading by example, Jim Hudson personally served on the Board of the Cultural Council, has been a Rotarian for 33 years with a 100% attendance record, and is the longest serving board member of the Oliver Gospel Mission to whom he donated six acres of land to be used for building a center for abused women and children. His philanthropy has also extended to charities including Sunshine for Children, the Heart Association, the National Kidney Foundation, the Salvation Army, the Oliver Gospel Mission, Meals on Wheels, and the Boy Scouts of America Indian Waters Council.

Jim Hudson Lexus, Augusta, GA. ▼

City of rivers, vistas, and dreams

Central Carolina Community Foundation

A Voice for Philanthropy in the Midlands

On September 25th, 1984, a group of Columbia's business leaders incorporated Central Carolina Community Foundation. For more than thirty years, the Foundation has served the Midlands by linking charitable people and businesses with areas of need. The Foundation provides stewardship for permanent endowments that enhance the lives of citizens in the Midlands,

▲ *Airport High School Student Government accepts 2012 Best of Philanthropy award for Student Group Champions.*

▶▲ *The Community Foundation manages various scholarship funds providing educational opportunities for future generations.*

▶ *Members of Safe Life Senior Ladies supporting Midlands Gives, the 24-hour online giving day.*

making the region a more caring and appealing place to live.

As a nonprofit serving donors and organizations in Calhoun, Clarendon, Fairfield, Kershaw, Lee, Lexington, Newberry, Orangeburg, Richland, Saluda, and Sumter counties, the Foundation acts as a vehicle for philanthropy for gifts and bequests received from individuals, families, businesses and organizations. The Foundation gives community members the tools and knowledge to invest in their community. In addition, the Community Foundation helps donors create legacies through bequests and trusts so that their charitable wishes live on long after they are gone.

A POWERFUL IMPACT ON COMMUNITY

"Since our founding, Central Carolina Community Foundation has been valued for our history of service and viewed as a trusted partner in philanthropy," stated JoAnn Turnquist, the Foundation's President and CEO. "Our assets

have grown from $25,000 to well over $108 million under the leadership of dedicated business and community leaders who have served on our board. With grants totaling $100 million to nonprofit organizations that range from the arts to animals, education to the environment, and health and well-being to human services, we have taken the leadership role in educating our community about the importance of giving locally.

We have become the catalyst for charitable growth in the Midlands of South Carolina. We connect people who want to give to causes they care about most."

By helping all donors pursue their personal charitable objectives, Central Carolina Community Foundation provides a unique opportunity for each donor to embrace their inner philanthropist.

Cultural Council of Richland & Lexington Counties

Promoting the Arts for South Carolina's Midlands

In May 1984, the Mayor of Columbia, Kirkman Finley, along with Dot Ryall and a handful of local business leaders met to establish an organization that would coordinate solicitation and distribution of donations to the arts in the Midlands area of the Palmetto State. At the time, there were only about three dozen not-for-profit arts organizations in the region. The founders felt it was necessary to have an organization whose mission would be to grow and expand the arts in the Midlands through the provision of general operating grants to the arts organizations that would allow them to use other funds to promote their programs.

The group established the Cultural Council of Richland and Lexington Counties following the business plan of other United Arts Funds across the country – a United Way approach to funding the arts. The Council's primary mission would be to nurture, develop, support, and promote the arts in Richland and Lexington Counties. Columbia was the perfect location for the organization's headquarters as the city is not only the capital of South Carolina, but is also county seat of Richland County and is centrally located for service to the Midlands.

GROWTH THROUGH SERVICE

In its three decades of service to the arts community of the state, the Cultural Council has evolved into a local arts agency providing grants, professional development, technical assistance and programs to build capacity of the arts organizations and individual artists. The Council's services are crucial to the growth of the arts in the region by providing general operating grants to arts organizations that allow them to use other funds to promote the programs. The experienced staff at the Council provides professional development opportunities and one-on-one technical assistance to arts administrators and individual artists to help them grow as arts providers. As artists themselves, the Council's staff understands the challenges facing the arts and can provide information on the latest national trends to assist them in overcoming those challenges. The Cultural Council is very active with Americans for the Arts, the national organization that provides support, research and information to local arts agencies.

The Council provides general operating grants to sixteen arts organizations annually. In addition, small arts organizations and individual artists apply for project grants ranging from $250 to $1,500, depending on funding availability. At least thirty project grants are awarded each year.

Today there are more than 130 not-for-profit arts organizations in the region due to the activities of the Council. These organizations provide over 1,500 full time jobs and approximately $50 million annually in economic impact.

In recognition of its service to the arts community of the Midlands region, the Cultural Council was presented with the Elizabeth O'Neill Verner Award from the South Carolina Arts Commission for its significant contributions to the arts in South Carolina.

▲ Local students assist in the creation of a mural on Decker Boulevard celebrating the International Corridor.

Guests of the annual Color the Arts festival admire the work of Columbia artists. ▼

The Cultural Council's annual event, Color the Arts, draws huge crowds of visitors and residents to celebrate the arts in Columbia. ▼

ENVIRO AgScience, Inc.

Where Business and Agriculture Equal Success

Dr. Louis B. Lynn decided in 1985 to launch ENVIRO AgScience, Inc. in Columbia. The decision was motivated by more than his dream to combine his horticultural expertise with his entrepreneurial acumen to create a residential landscaping company. Lynn envisioned a socially responsible business that would provide employment opportunities in his community

and enable him to pay what he felt was his "civic rent." During its almost three decades of service, his business has done exactly that.

A native of Darlington County, Dr. Lynn built on his Bachelor's and Master's degrees in horticulture from Clemson University and earned his doctorate in the same field from the University of Maryland. He felt that launching his business in South Carolina's capital would enable him to bid on a multitude of projects sponsored by various agencies across the Palmetto State. His reputation for quality work and his willingness to accept the challenges relating to the federal government's detailed criteria for firms bidding on federal projects, including security, drug screening of employees and the necessary paperwork, led to rapid growth and expansion.

Lynn's staff of professionals was soon being chosen by firms such as BMW, Roche Carolina, Clemson University, Morris College, Benedict College, DuPont and a host of others. ENVIRO provided the design and landscaping for projects ranging from Department of Energy's Savannah River Site, Main Street Streetscape in Columbia, NCO Academy at Fort Jackson, Veterans Administration National Cemetery, Governors School for the Arts and many other signature developments. With these signature projects on the company resume, ENVIRO AgScience, Inc. soon became the largest minority-owned landscape firm in South Carolina.

Dr. Lynn was quick to broaden the initial scope of his business to include construction and

construction management projects. ENVIRO AgScience, Inc. was soon managing large-scale undertakings for public schools, public housing, municipal buildings and clients in the manufacturing sector. The firm has put its signature on numerous new construction projects such as the Columbia Convention Center, the University of South Carolina Colonial Center and over a dozen K-12 public schools. It has also successfully completed numerous initiatives for the federal government, including Department of Defense contracts for new construction or renovations at Fort Benning, Fort Stewart, Fort Jackson, Camp Lejeune and Fort Bragg.

"We provide construction and construction management services for customers in highly demanding sectors, including government, military, hospitality, automotive, education, and manufacturing," Dr. Lynn stated. "But what really sets us apart is the way we work, the way we support and collaborate with our customers. In short, our business is as much about building relationships as it is about buildings."

REALIZING A DREAM

ENVIRO AgScience, Inc. is headquartered on a 12-acre campus in Columbia. In addition, the company, which employs 70 people, also maintains offices in Atlanta. Dr. Lynn is pursuing international status by exploring opportunities to manage construction projects in Africa, Canada and Brazil.

The company's quality work, attention to detail and commitment to personalized service to each client have led to numerous industry awards. In 2011,

Dr. Louis B. Lynn, President and CEO

Richland County Recreation Commission, Columbia, S.C.

ENVIRO was named by the U.S. Department of Commerce as the Regional Minority Construction Firm of the Year. The following year, the company was recognized as number four of the "Top 25 Fastest Growing Companies in South Carolina." Later in the same year, Dr. Lynn was feted in Washington, D.C., again by the U.S. Department of Commerce, and received the Ronald H. Brown Leadership Award, a prestigious honor recognizing exceptional leaders who have made great strides in creating diversity in the public or private sector.

As his company has evolved and expanded, Dr. Lynn feels privileged to have realized the achievement of another goal that he had set for himself and for his business – providing job opportunities for local people. "We've been able to help more people as we've grown over the years," he noted in an interview in 2011. "When we line up new business, my first thought is 'I can hire some more people.'"

While the accolades ENVIRO AgScience, Inc. has garnered from its industry peers are certainly rewarding, probably the greatest reward Dr. Lynn has received is having seen his children, Adrienne Lynn, Dr. Krystal

University of South Carolina Colonial Arena, Columbia, S.C.

Conner, and Bryan Lynn, join in the family business. Ms. Lynn, an engineer and former executive with the Campbell Soup Company, and Dr. Conner, a registered pharmacist, both left successful careers to join their father in the business he founded and are located in the firm's Atlanta office. Bryan Lynn serves as a manager in the landscape division in Columbia.

The family business today remains focused on service to their clients while at the same time returning something to the communities which Dr. Lynn feel have been so supportive of him. He continues to "pay his civic rent" in numerous ways, including serving on the Clemson Board of Trustees (six four-year terms), the South Carolina Workforce Investment Board, the State Chamber of Commerce, the Columbia Chamber of Commerce, South Carolina's Governor's School for Science and Mathematics, the Palmetto Agribusiness Council, the Midlands Business Leadership Council, the State Museum Foundation, and many others. A devout Christian, he continues to daily live his business mission statement as stated in Proverbs 16:3, "Commit thy works unto the Lord and thy thoughts shall be established."

Dr. Lynn with ENVIRO Vice Presidents and daughters, Dr. Krystal Conner (left) and Mrs. Adrienne Lynn Sienkowski, (right) accepting 4th ranked SC Fastest Growing Company Award.

Polo Road Elementary under construction, Columbia, South Carolina

Columbia Metropolitan Convention Center, Columbia, South Carolina

Hussey, Gay, Bell & De Young

A Tradition of Exceptional Service and Solutions

The engineering consulting and architectural design professionals at Hussey, Gay, Bell & DeYoung (HGBD) will soon be celebrating 60 years of providing exceptional service and solutions to meet the needs of a broad range of satisfied clients. The firm's Columbia office is located on Assembly Street between Lady and Gervais in the historic 1905 South Carolina National Guard Armory Building, formerly occupied by the legendary Cromer's P-Nuts. The building was purchased and completely renovated by the firm's CEO, G. Holmes Bell, IV, and his father, Gus Bell, III. Today the firm has evolved into a family of six specialized companies with more than 100 professional staff members with additional offices in the heart of Charleston, South Carolina; Savannah and Atlanta, Georgia; and Riyadh, Saudi Arabia.

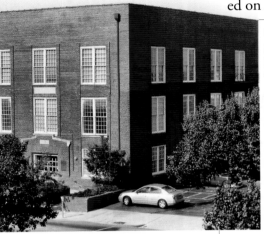

▲ The firm's Columbia office is located on Assembly Street between Lady and Gervais in the historic 1905 South Carolina National Guard Armory Building, formerly occupied by the legendary Cromer's P-Nuts.

Consistently ranked an ENR Top 500 Design Firm, Hussey, Gay, Bell & DeYoung has provided professional engineering and architectural services in South Carolina and throughout the Southeast since 1958. The firm provides full design services in the fields of transportation, drainage, civil, water and wastewater systems, solid waste, site development, master planning, landscape architecture, geotechnical engineering, environmental engineering and surveying, architecture, and planning services in addition to program management.

An award-winning project, HGBD received an ACEC Engineering Excellence award for work performed on a 200+ acre site for Boeing's new 787 airplane manufacturing facility. ▼

THE NEXT GENERATION OF LEADERSHIP AT HGBD

In January 2013, G. Holmes Bell, IV, PE, became Chairman of all HGBD companies. His father, Gus Bell, III, PE, became Chairman in 1986 and served through December 2012. Today, Gus Bell, III remains active in the business as Chairman Emeritus, spearheading HGBD's South Carolina business development.

"I literally grew up in this business," says G. Holmes Bell, IV, PE. "I began working on our survey crews the summer after seventh grade. Dad wanted me to respect hard work at an early age

and to learn the business from the ground up. It has given me a greater appreciation for our business and the services we provide."

Since the firm's inception, HGBD has provided engineering and architectural design services in 36 states and 19 countries across the globe.

Evidence of the design and engineering expertise of HGBD is demonstrated domestically and internationally - from Palmetto Dunes Resort on Hilton Head Island, the Boeing Company Expansion in North Charleston, the SCDOT Camden Truck By-Pass and SCDOT SC-7 Bridge Replacement to Rousakis Plaza on River Street in Savannah, Georgia, and the massive JCB operations on I-95. In addition, HGBD Arabia is wrapping up two of its largest projects to date – designing 33 wastewater treatment facilities from the ground up in two diverse areas of Saudi Arabia.

"We are so fortunate to have the most talented and dedicated professionals working here at HGBD," Holmes Bell notes. "I have no doubt we can keep the firm growing and performing to the highest level of standards. As we do so, we will also continue our long and established history of professional and civic involvement working with various civic and charitable organizations and serving on numerous boards to improve the quality of life for the people in the communities we serve."

▶ A signature HGBD project, the historic waterfront revitalization of Rousakis Plaza is an Urban Renewal Project located within the section of Savannah designated as a Registered National Historic Landmark by the United States Department of the Interior.
—Photo by Geoff L. Johnson

Columbia Metropolitan Magazine

Columbia's City Magazine

The cover of Columbia Metropolitan Magazine's September 2013 issue.

Co-owners and publishers, Emily and Henry Clay. ▼

Each month, approximately 100,000 people in the Richland and Lexington Counties metropolitan area turn to the pages of *Columbia Metropolitan* Magazine to stay abreast of the latest in what is new and exciting in the largest city in South Carolina and the capital of the Palmetto State.

While the magazine focuses primarily on the Columbia metropolitan area, readers throughout the Midlands region of South Carolina regularly pick up the magazine for its insightful writing, stunning photography and broad focus on events in those areas.

Founded in 1990 by Emily and Henry Clay (Georgia and Louisiana natives respectively), the publication has become the "go-to" source on what is hot in dining, business, home and garden, the arts, health and wellness, education, community events and a myriad of amenities that helped establish Columbia's reputation as "The Capital of Southern Hospitality."

The couple's journey to their present position as publishers of *Columbia Metropolitan* was a circuitous one. After graduating from Washington and Lee University with a degree in history, Henry married Emily, who graduated from Hollins College with a BA in English, and the couple traveled and lived in far away New Zealand before returning to their Southern roots.

With the dust still on their boots from farm life in Georgia, Emily and Henry moved to Columbia in March 1990 to launch *Columbia Metropolitan* Magazine. Working with their partners at *Augusta Magazine*, they premiered the first issue in Columbia in June of that same year.

"Our goal was to showcase what was best about the city we had both come to love," Henry explains. "There are so many things about Columbia that account for the exceptional quality of life we experience here. Naturally, we were concerned about how such a magazine focusing on local life would be received. We were in our twenties and were well aware of the big step we were taking to go out on our own. But we were convinced that our business plan was solid and a high-quality publication focusing on the Midlands would fill a much-needed niche locally. From the outset, we used only the highest quality paper, photography, writing and graphic design. We became known for thought-provoking writing, exceptional photography and topics of interest to local people as well as visitors to our area. We grew from a quarterly publication to our present position of producing ten issues annually. In addition, we now print about 20,000 copies of each issue that reaches about 100,000 readers. We feel very fortunate regarding the Columbia community's reception of the publication regarding our loyal and growing readership."

A RECIPE FOR SUCCESS

Henry Clay is quick to point to the talented staff at *Columbia Metropolitan* as the cornerstone of the continued success and growth of the magazine. They have been relentless in ferreting out the best the city has to offer in every aspect of local life. The "Best of Columbia" feature allows residents and out-of-town visitors to find what readers have voted as the best places to go locally to find everything from a romantic dinner to a comfortable coffee house or yogurt bar. From selecting the perfect apartment complex to tuning in to the best radio station. From locating the best doctors and dentists in Columbia to the most popular toy stores for holiday presents.

Readers have also grown accustomed to perusing the magazine's 140 or more pages for tips on planting the perfect spring garden. Other articles might profile a local couple's efforts to renovate a century-old home while retaining its historic heritage. Still others offer advice on selecting the best cabernet to serve with a certain pork tenderloin at a dinner party. Regular features spotlighting the local arts community include everything from the seasonal schedule of the South Carolina Philharmonic to the opening of an exhibit showcasing the work of a Columbia artist.

Henry also points to the focus at *Columbia Metropolitan* for staying abreast of the latest advances in technology and incorporating them into their magazine to remain on the cutting edge of the constantly changing environment in the publication industry. "In 2010, we came to realize that our readers wanted more from us than just the printed version of their city magazine each month," he noted. "We'd been giving them the print publication for two decades and four years ago we began giving them even more with online media.

"The magazine's loyal readership can now sign up for our weekly newsletters, like us on Facebook, and follow us on Twitter, Instagram and Pinterest. We are using the various communication tools to keep our readers informed about what to do, where to go and how to find fabulous deals around town.

"We are extremely excited and encouraged about all of these opportunities to continue to strengthen our relationships with our dedicated readers and loyal advertisers."

Emily and Henry Clay agree that their greatest reward from the successful launch and evolution of their magazine has been in highlighting the people and organizations that improve the quality of life in the city that they love.

▲ Columbia Metropolitan Magazine *is available on all of your devices through* columbianmetro.com.

Each issue of Columbia Metropolitan *features at least one beautiful Columbia home.* ▼

KICKING IT IN THE KITCHEN

Saucy new styles

By Natalie Meggs
Photography by Robert Clark

The Dunbars

Built/Renovated: 2013/2014 by Patrick Dunbar of
    Dunbar Builders
Designer: Gretchen Opgenorth of Gretchen O. Studio
Cabinets: Randy Schrader of Schrader Kitchens
    & Furniture
Countertops: Leathered Granite with a Cherry Wood
    Chopping Block island from Real Value, Inc. Marble
    & Granite Fabricators
Backsplash: Wedgwood subway tile from The Tile
    Center, Inc.
Flooring: Birch hand scraped hardwood flooring
Sink: Porcelain Farmhouse sink from Hughes Supply
Appliances: S&G Builders Appliances
Lighting: Pendant Lighting over the sink from
    Restoration Hardware; above the island from
    Urban Electric Company (Charleston)
Color Schemes: Blue/cream/neutrals

Photo by Paul Ringger

C O L U M B I A

The Wilson Group of Companies, Inc.

Proven Strategies For Achieving Financial Success

Skip Wilson founded The Wilson Group of Companies, Inc. in 1993 as a financial and insurance services firm committed to helping his clients realize their current and long-term financial goals. The firm now provides a wide range of financial products, including investments, employee benefits and individual insurance, as well as, property and casualty insurance encompassing products for auto, home, boat, business, and more along with

▲ Wilson offers one-on-one consultation meetings in the areas of retirement, insurance and business planning.

▶ Each employee of The Wilson Group offers specialized services to clients:
Ann Overcash – INVESTMENTS
Barbara Guyton – LIFE, DISABILITY INCOME, LONG TERM CARE
Rose Stuck – PROPERTY AND CASUALTY INSURANCE
Skip Wilson – PRESIDENT AND CEO
Camber Moore – PAYROLL AND BOOKKEEPING
Donna Lewis – HEALTH BENEFITS

prepaid legal plans, identity theft coverage, bookkeeping and payroll services. The Wilson Group's success over the years has been defined by its dedication to providing the most up-to-date products as well as forming strategic alliances with some of the most reputable investment firms and insurance carriers in the industry.

From the outset, Wilson realized that finding the right solution for his clients' personal or business needs required a sharp focus on the circumstances of each individual client's unique situation. He adopted a needs-based approach based on a four-step process of analyzing, recommending, implementing, and reviewing each individual strategy to ensure that his clients are on the right course to achieve their goals and remain on that course as life unfolds.

- ANALYZE. Before recommending any product or service,

Wilson asks questions and obtains a clear understanding of the client's financial goals and objectives.

- RECOMMEND. Wilson next provides suggestions to fill in the gaps so the client can choose the products best suited for his or her unique situation.

- IMPLEMENT. If the client is satisfied with his recommendations, Wilson works to implement those strategies and secure the required products and services to help ensure financial freedom.

- REVIEW. Because our financial situations change over time, Wilson provides periodic reviews to help clients monitor their strategies in place and their capacity to continuously meet the stated goals.

A PATH TO THE FUTURE

Few decisions we make in our lives are as important as choosing the right person to trust with creating and managing our own personal wealth. Ensuring that we have the financial resources to meet our individual goals, whether planning for college, protecting our business, or preparing for a comfortable retirement.

Navigating the waters of financial security is never easy. The road is often complicated, time consuming, and difficult—perhaps even a bit overwhelming. Whether preparing for a milestone life event, such as retirement or the sale of a business, or simply looking for financial protection for the future, The Wilson Group is the name that clients have trusted for over two decades for unsurpassed attention, insight, and guidance.

"I take the time to understand your needs, explain different options to you and earn your trust before offering possible solutions," Wilson states. "By working with me, you can take meaningful, manageable steps toward developing an integrated strategy to help achieve a secure financial future."

Midlands Authority for Conventions, Sports & Tourism

Introducing the World to "The New Southern Hot Spot"

With four million visitors traveling to Columbia, South Carolina each year to discover its world-class attractions, breathtaking natural locales and exciting downtown scene full of restaurants, shopping and nightlife, the region has quickly grown into "The New Southern Hot Spot" for leisure and business travel. In promoting the area's "hot spots," Columbia attracts niche audiences while also opening itself up to a more diverse group of visitors who seek different qualities in a destination.

"The New Culinary Hot Spot" reflects the unique Southern flavor that can be found in the exceptional dishes at area restaurants. From fine dining to barbecue joints to eateries featuring locally-sourced ingredients, each establishment provides a culinary experience that is Columbia through and through.

The rich history of "The New Historic Hot Spot" can be explored by visiting Historic Columbia properties like the Woodrow Wilson Family Home, touring the South Carolina State House, or participating in the Columbia '63 Civil Rights walking tour along Main Street.

The impressive collection at the Columbia Museum of Art, quirky public sculptures, and abundance of galleries located throughout the region all contribute to the burgeoning scene and beauty of "The New Artistic Hot Spot."

Families can make lasting memories together in "The New Kid-Friendly Hot Spot." Riverbanks Zoo & Garden, EdVenture Children's Museum, and the South Carolina State Museum foster family fun in innovative environments.

Whether kayaking on one of the area's three rivers, hiking and camping in Congaree National Park, boating on Lake Murray, or biking through Harbison State Forest, there are many thrills to be had in "The New Adventure Hot Spot."

Together, these "hot spots," as well as the many visitors and meeting attendees choosing to come here every year, make Columbia "The New Southern Hot Spot" and the Midlands Authority for Conventions, Sports & Tourism is here to let the world know.

MIDLANDS AUTHORITY

Overseeing the Columbia Metropolitan Convention and Visitors Bureau (CVB), Columbia Metropolitan Convention Center (CMCC), Columbia Regional Sports Council (CRSC), and Columbia Regional Visitors Center (CRVC), the Midlands Authority is a helpful resource for visitors and meeting/event planners traveling to the Columbia region and strives to tout the many offerings and amenities available throughout the area on regional, national, and international platforms.

For more than thirty years, the CVB has built lasting relationships with community partners and worked together with them to market the Columbia area to visitors and meeting planners. Serving as ambassadors to the region, the CVB delivers a helping hand to those interested in traveling to Columbia by answering questions, providing quality information, offering suggestions on things to do, and booking hotel rooms and event venues.

"The Midlands Authority serves as a primary driver of economic development through tourism for the Columbia region," states Bill Ellen, President and CEO of the Authority. "Focusing on leisure travel, meetings and conventions, and participant-based sporting events, we strategically work to increase the number of individuals visiting and staying in the area annually. Over the last ten years, we've redesigned our overall approach to bring the key areas of the Authority- the CVB, CRSC and CMCC - under one roof, providing a seamless and unified message about the region's offerings. Columbia is constantly growing, developing and changing and we love to have visitors experience all that we have to offer."

The Authority is a dynamic destination marketing organization for the greater Columbia region - Richland County, Lexington County, and the City of Columbia. Visitors and meeting planners can find additional area information at columbiacvb.com, in the Official Columbia Visitors Guide, and at the Columbia Regional Visitors Center.

▲ *Kayakers on the Congaree River.*

All photos courtesy of the Columbia Metropolitan Convention & Visitors Bureau.

◄ *Zoo – Feeding giraffes at Riverbanks Zoo & Garden.*

The Columbia, SC downtown skyline. ▼

Photo by Paul Ringger

C O L U M B I A

Thermal Technologies, Inc.

Quality, Innovation, Service, & Support

Thermal Technologies, Inc. was founded in 1987 in suburban Philadelphia, Pennsylvania as a cold storage construction firm specializing in freezer, cooler and fruit storage warehouses and dock facilities. Co-founder Jim Lentz was acutely aware of problems with banana quality control at that time and wanted to launch a business that would pioneer the development of a new type of banana ripening room.

He did exactly that.

AN IDEA BECOMES REALITY

Lentz and his wife Deb soon realized that their new business was rapidly growing beyond its original dimensions. Important decisions and changes had to be made as the company grew, first and foremost being the search for a suitable place to relocate as Thermal Tech outgrew its Philadelphia headquarters. After serious consideration of several different locations along the Eastern Seaboard, they decided on a facility in Blythewood, South Carolina. The location had ample room for expansion in a bustling, pro-business region with plenty of transportation options. The move in 2002 was facilitated by the City of Columbia and the state of South Carolina, both of whom played a proactive role in making sure the transition was as smooth as possible.

Once in South Carolina, sales of the TarpLess Ripening Room continued to grow. This sustained growth led to a recent $1.2 million expansion of the manufacturing facility, nearly doubling the size of the plant.

As the industry leader in banana ripening room design and installation, Thermal Technologies is now busy installing the rooms it manufactures at major retail distribution facilities from Maine to California and from Canada to Mexico.

Thermal Tech continues to set the standard in pressurized ripening for the entire industry with the most advanced technology, groundbreaking, patented designs, unsurpassed ripening knowledge and unbeatable customer service. Today, Thermal Tech's patented "TarpLess" ripening room system is the most widely used in the industry, ripening over 100 million pounds of bananas each day, or 70 percent of all bananas processed across the United States, Canada, and Mexico.

Now used by nine of the ten largest national grocery retail chains in North America, every TarpLess ripening room is manufactured right here in the Midlands at Thermal Tech's corporate headquarters and factory in Blythewood.

Thermal Tech employs 23 full and part-time workers from across the region. The company is a proud member of the Columbia and South Carolina Chambers of Commerce. Jim Lentz was presented an Ambassador for Economic Development Award in April 2013 by South Carolina Governor Nikki Haley and Bobby Hitt, South Carolina's Secretary of Commerce, in honor of Thermal Tech's facility expansion project.

Being part of the community and supporting local causes plays an important role in the lives of Jim and Deb Lentz. "South Carolina and the Columbia region have been very good to us and we feel it's important to give back," say Jim, "not just by providing jobs, but by supporting the local organizations and people who make this such a great place to live and work."

◀ *Thermal Tech President Jim Lentz (center) receives an Ambassador for Economic Development Award on April 30th, 2013 in honor of Thermal Tech's facility expansion project. The award is being presented by South Carolina Governor Nikki Haley (left) and Bobby Hitt, South Carolina Secretary of Commerce (right).*

▲ *Inside Thermal Tech's 15,000 sq. ft. factory expansion.*

Thermal Technologies Corporate Headquarters & Factory, Blythewood, SC. ▼

CCC Group, Inc.

Nationally Recognized Excellence Through Quality and Safety

In 1947 Merle Huebner and George Guthrie founded CCC Group, Inc., destined to become a nationally recognized industrial construction company. While many of the partners' early successes were in commercial construction, it would not be long before their industrial projects far outnumbered their commercial jobs. Just two years after its founding, CCC Group completed its first project for Alcoa, who has remained a loyal client ever since. Today, CCC Group is primarily a constructor for heavy industry.

Huebner and Guthrie passed along the leadership and ownership of the company to their sons, Arthur, Kenneth, and Douglas Huebner and Clifton Guthrie. Ownership of the company was extended in 2004 with the initiation of an employee stock ownership program (ESOP). A third generation of Guthrie and Huebner sons is carrying on the legacy of the founders as employees of the company holding various positions of different levels and working in different divisions of CCC Group.

▲ *Two Crane Lift at Gypsum Wallboard Plant.*

A STRATEGY OF GROWTH

CCC Group provides quality construction, fabrication, maintenance, and engineering, services to a wide range of market sectors, including:

- Mining and metals
- Oil, gas, and chemicals
- Power
- General manufacturing
- International
- Detention systems

In the course of the almost seven decades of its existence, CCC Group has focused on being a relationship driven industrial contractor driven to excel in safely performing projects and delivering results that consistently meet or exceed client expectations. The company's skilled professionals accomplish these results through the employment of key personnel who both live and work in Columbia along with strong corporate support and backing. Since CCC Group is an employee owned company, all personnel, including project managers, supervisors, and support staff, strive to consistently deliver excellent results.

CCC Group's growth strategy is to expand by establishing regional offices to serve regional markets. The company had completed a number of projects in Georgia, South Carolina, and North Carolina for clients including Alcoa, Commercial Metals, Duke, MeadWestvaco, and Pepsi prior to 2003. Based on its experience in the area, CCC Group opened a regional office in Columbia in 2003 to service the east coast. Since that time the Columbia office has completed projects throughout the Southeast and Mid-Atlantic Regions.

AN IMPRINT ON THE REGION

CCC Group's South Carolina Regional Office now services cement, lime, chemical, power, mineral processing, specialty chemical, steel, and aluminum industries.

Rotary Lime Kiln Installation. ▼

Wood Pellet Terminal Facility. ▼

The primary service area for the regional office includes the Southeast and Mid-Atlantic regions.

While the Columbia office numbers twenty full-time employees and normally employs more than 200 craft workers, CCC Group as a whole provides jobs for approximately 500 full-time managers, supervisors, and support staff along with 2,000 craft employees.

"CCC Group established its Columbia office by bringing a small core group into Columbia," states Richard Swartout, the company's Division Manager. "We expanded by a combination of bringing in additional personnel and hiring locally. We provide good jobs that add to the local economy, and our staff is involved locally in churches, civic organizations, and youth sports. We have found Columbia to be a great place to live and raise our families by combining the amenities of a larger city with Southern hospitality and small town friendliness."

The decision to expand into Columbia proved to be a fortuitous move. In 2003, while still in its infancy, the South Carolina Regional office managed to produce $1 million in volume. Ten years later, with a top-notch core team, established operations, and solid roots in the area, CCC Group's 2013 volume totaled $25 million and included 205,000 man-hours worked. Although the jobs that are managed from the Columbia office span multiple states along the east coast, the company has a core team that works on a daily basis in South Carolina and is constantly seeking opportunities to provide industrial construction services to local industries.

High profile projects that bear the CCC Group signature are many:

- General construction of a non-woven manufacturing facility for Jacob Holm
- Lime processing plant for Martin Marietta Magnesia Specialties
- Wallboard manufacturing facility for National Gypsum
- Cement plant modernization for Keystone
- Wood pellet export terminal for Enviva
- Magnetic slag separation system installation for BASF
- Lime hydration system installation for Lhoist North America

- FGD project for Georgia Power Plant Scherer

In the completion of these and numerous other projects, CCC Group has garnered numerous awards, including the Southern Company President's Safety Award in 2010 and 2013, and a ranking of 121 among the top 400 contractors in the U.S. by Engineering News Record. In addition, the company consistently receives top national rankings among contractors in the chemical plants, power and hydro plants, mining, industrial process, and marine and port facilities sectors.

"We are proud to be known as a relationship driven industrial contractor that consistently meets or exceeds the safety, quality, budget, and schedule expectations of our clients," Swartout adds. "Our company continues to focus on developing and maintaining lasting relationships with our clients that result in a high percentage of repeat business."

▲ *Cement Plant Preheater Tower.*

Gypsum Wallboard Plant. ▼

Truck Unloading Hopper. ▼

Alliance Consulting Engineers, Inc.

On Time. On Budget. On Your Side.

The Proclamation by the Columbia City Council marking May 10, 2014 as "Alliance Consulting Engineers Day" and the South Carolina House of Representatives Resolution to recognize Alliance Consulting Engineers, Inc. for its "significant contributions to statewide economic growth and development" was the highlight of the celebration of the engineering company's tenth anniversary of service. The honors underscored the role Alliance Consulting

▲ *Taylor Street Parking Garage, City of Columbia, S.C.*

▼ *Lexington Medical Center, Lexington County, S.C.*

Engineers, Inc. has played in local and regional economic development in the state with its assistance in projects totaling $8 billion in industrial investment and 24,000 new jobs in South Carolina.

The proclamations went on to commend the company for its excellence in providing engineering services to the City of Columbia and to communities throughout the entire state and the Southeast, highlighting the $100 million in grants and low-interest loans it has helped its clients secure in order to finance key infrastructure and industrial projects. Alliance was also praised for its dedication to community service and especially its efforts to give back to the City of Columbia.

Pursuit of a Dream

A native of Sri Lanka, Deepal S. Eliatamby founded Alliance Consulting Engineers, Inc. in 2004 on the concept of providing unsurpassed, in-depth personal involvement on today's complex engineering projects. The hands-on approach and meticulous attention to detail that he envisioned for every project that his company accepted would begin from conceptual planning and continue through to final design, permitting, and construction. Using traditional business practices and the latest technology, Eliatamby's mission for Alliance Consulting Engineers, Inc. was to demonstrate the company's commitment to every client through responsiveness, experience, and quality results.

Eliatamby's formula for success has proven to be right on target. The young man who arrived in the United States with two bags and a backpack now heads a company of 75 professionals with five offices in South and North Carolina. In addition to the company's corporate headquarters at the Midlands Regional Office in Columbia, Alliance Consulting Engineers, Inc. also maintains their Lowcountry Regional Office in Bluffton, South Carolina; the Upstate Regional Office in Greenville, South Carolina; the Charleston Regional Office in Charleston, South Carolina; and the Charlotte Regional Office in Charlotte, North Carolina.

During the last decade, Alliance Consulting Engineers has grown into one of the state's largest civil and environmental engineering firms. As the firm celebrates its tenth anniversary, company leaders look to the promise of growth on the horizon.

"We are thrilled and honored to reach the milestone of our tenth anniversary, especially considering the economic challenges our nation has experienced in the last decade," states Eliatamby. "We believe our success is a testament to the talented people we have on our team and our great clients who have let us use our skills to streamline their projects and save them time and money."

To date, Alliance has worked on more than 900 projects, spanning all 46 counties in South Carolina and many projects in North Carolina, Georgia and other Southeastern States. One area of concentration has been economic

development and working with companies that are building new facilities or expanding existing ones. High-profile companies Alliance has assisted include Continental Tire, Nephron Pharmaceuticals Corporation, Adidas, BMW, QVC, Home Depot, Monster.com, Amazon.com, Toray Industries and numerous others.

Alliance has also assisted cities and counties in the Southeast with infrastructure projects. These projects include more than 200 miles of water and wastewater lines, numerous water and wastewater treatment facilities, speculative industrial buildings, industrial site certifications and master plans, and roadway plans.

While the size of the operation has continued to grow over its decade in existence, the core values on which Eliatamby founded his business have remained constant. "Our three core values - responsiveness, quality control and added value – are what separate us from other engineering firms," he notes. "Alliance's responsiveness is supported by its state-of-the-art equipment, which also helps with work quality. We have a very strict policy on quality control, and we always try to bring something to the table. We want to add value to every project we touch."

A TRADITION OF SERVICE

The professionals at Alliance Consulting Engineers, Inc. take great pride in providing a complete range of civil and environmental engineering services to a wide range of clients.

MASTER PLANNING AND DESIGN

Project personnel from Alliance Consulting Engineers, Inc. provide a complete range of services for the site design and planning of industrial sites. The company's design specialists understand the unique infrastructure

demands associated with the development of industrial sites. From family-owned operations to facilities of over two million square feet for Fortune 500 companies, Alliance personnel have been involved with the development of numerous industrial sites throughout the Southeastern United States.

CONSTRUCTION SERVICES

Once the planning, engineering design and permitting are completed, Alliance professionals can provide construction administration and observation services during the construction phase of the project. Construction administration and observation are critical to assure that the construction proceeds in accordance with the expectations of the client and in accordance with the permitted conditions of the particular project.

SOLID WASTE MANAGEMENT

Since its inception, Alliance Consulting Engineers, Inc. has assisted municipalities, counties and individuals with solid waste management services. The company's

solid waste related services are multifaceted ranging from planning to post-closure care.

By staying current with ever-changing regulations established by both state and federal agencies, the engineering design and permitting proficiency of Alliance Consulting Engineers,

▲ McDaniels Acura, Richland County, S.C.

Inc. personnel have resulted in the successful permitting of numerous solid waste related facilities. Additionally, the company has assisted South Carolina counties with maintaining solid waste management plans to govern the solid waste facilities within the county as required by regulatory agencies.

▼ Malls & Shopping Centers.

▲ Sarah Collins Special Needs Program Car Wash in Greenville, S.C.

▲ Adopt a Highway – 12th Street Extension, Lexington County, S.C.

GRANTS

The grant professionals at Alliance Consulting Engineers, Inc. have extensive experience in accessing grant and funding programs ranging from Community Development Block Grants and Economic Development Administration Funds to State Revolving Fund Programs of the Environmental Protection Agency.

WITH AN EYE TO THE FUTURE

Deepal Eliatamby and his staff appreciate the support the company has received over the years from their clients and look forward to continuing the business relationships that have been the cornerstone of their success. That commitment is evidenced in the recent expansion of their corporate headquarters to better serve the many clients who have put their faith in the myriad services provided by Alliance Consulting Engineers, Inc.

In June 2014, the company began expansion of its corporate headquarters which have been located on Main Street since the company's founding. One of several large companies to call downtown home, the expansion increases the firm's corporate footprint to 17,000 square feet - nearly an entire floor in Capitol Center Tower, making it one of the top ten largest tenants in the 25-story building that is also the tallest building in the state.

The expansion ensures that Alliance Consulting Engineers, Inc. will have the physical space to support its growing staff, to better serve its clients, and to promote economic and business development in the area.

"Our commitment to the Midlands and South Carolina is further strengthened as we continue to grow to serve our clients and be the largest locally owned civil and environmental engineering company based in the region," Eliatamby noted. "As we look to the next ten years, we will continue to expand our footprint to better serve our clients."

PEER RECOGNITION

The company's record of excellence and integrity has earned it numerous industry awards and accolades, including:

- On May 5, 2014, Alliance Consulting Engineers, Inc. was ranked by Engineering News-Record magazine (ENR), as one of the top ten design firms in South Carolina and one of the top

▼ Adidas Distribution Facility, Spartanburg County.

▼ Wastewater Treatment Plant, Orangeburg County.

▲ *The Mayor's Isabel Law Breast Cancer Breakfast.*

75 design firms within the Southeastern United States including Florida, Georgia, North Carolina, and South Carolina.

- In November 2013, Alliance Consulting Engineers, Inc. was named one of the fastest growing companies in South Carolina by Capital Corporation, Integrated Media Publishing and others in the annual "25 Fastest-Growing Companies" listing. Now in its thirteenth year, the "25 Fastest-Growing Companies" competition recognizes the achievements of top-performing private and publicly-owned companies that have contributed to South Carolina's economy through exceptional increases in revenues and employment.

- Also in 2013, Alliance Consulting Engineers, Inc. was ranked in the annual Grant Thornton "South Carolina 100" as one of South Carolina's 100 largest privately held companies.

"We are very pleased to be ranked on the 'South Carolina 100'," Eliatamby stated on receiving the award. "Being named one of South Carolina's largest privately held companies is an honor, and we are very grateful to our clients for their ongoing support and for helping us earn this honor. As we complete our tenth year of client service, we look forward to even more growth in South Carolina and the Southeastern U.S."

In an ongoing effort to return something to the communities that have been so supportive of the company he founded, Eliatamby encourages his employees to volunteer their time outside the office. "Find something that you are passionate about, whether it's economic development or working with charitable organizations – that makes each of us a better person, which makes for a better company and helps make our communities stronger," he encourages them.

His employees have done exactly that. They now provide support to more than a dozen civic and charitable organizations ranging from the United Way of the Midlands, the Service Dog Institute of Greenville, and Bluffton Lions Club to the USO, Isabel's Law Breast Cancer Breakfast, and Big Brothers and Big Sisters of the Midlands among others.

◄◄ *(photo in margin page opposite)*
John W. Matthews Industrial Park
Water Tank, Orangeburg County, S.C.

▼ *Timken Sports Complex, Union County, S.C.*

▼ *Amazon.com Fulfillment Center, Lexington County, S.C.*

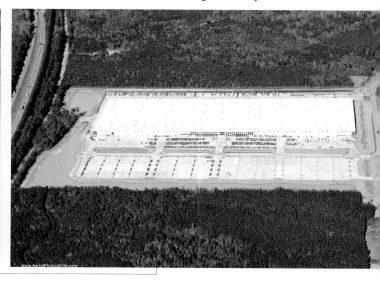

Brownstone Construction Group

Delivering Quality Projects On Time and Within Budget

Brownstone Construction Group has been delivering program and construction management services in the southeast since 2005 and has established itself as a premier minority-owned Construction Management and Architectural Design firm in the State of South Carolina. With over $200 million of completed construction experience,

▲ *Haut Gap Middle School - Johns Island, SC*

Brownstone has successfully provided committed and competent services for Owners. One of the key drivers of Brownstone's success is our commitment to exceeding clients' expectations and our ability to deliver on our promise of on-time and on-budget performance.

Darla Moore School of Business - Image Courtesy of USC ▼

PROVIDING THE RIGHT SOLUTIONS FOR OUR CLIENTS

Our staff is very familiar with all facets of agency/construction program management services including scheduling, cost estimating, value engineering, site management, procurement and document control. We focus on and specialize in being an advocate for the Owner and acting as an extension of their staff. The vast majority of our experience has been in this type of role, and we are diligent about maintaining our reputation as dedicated Program Managers and Owner Advocates. Brownstone brings superb facility program management expertise, local knowledge, management tools, knowledge of the South Carolina market, and a complete understanding of compliance with all applicable laws, guidelines and requirements. We are not the biggest firm, and we do not pursue everything. We focus on the market sectors and regions that we can fully support and in which we are experienced and successful. With

this mindset, we are proud of our repeat clients here in Columbia as well as in Charleston, Dillon, and Savannah, Georgia.

During a recent interview, Dale Collier gave the following response to a question regarding the most rewarding aspect of being the President of Brownstone Construction Group: "In our attempts to be client-oriented, we strive to provide the right solutions for our clients. This focus has allowed us to gain the trust of those who've entrusted Brownstone to provide construction, program management and architectural design services. We are proud to have a listing of satisfied, and even repeat, clients who've rehired our team to provide additional services. Working and connecting with people of various backgrounds and capabilities has been very rewarding. In most cases, clients retain our services for a specific period of time, and we provide consulting services in an area for which they are unfamiliar. Establishing and maintaining the confidence of our clients has given us the opportunity to secure work in other locales based on positive references received from others."

ESTABLISHING A LOCAL PRESENCE

During our time in Columbia, Brownstone has worked to establish our presence in the area by providing competent and legitimate services for our clients. Significant projects to date that we've been involved with include Richland School District Two's Center for Achievement and the recently completed University of South Carolina's Darla Moore School of Business. On the heels of the completion of the Business School, Brownstone will continue

its relationship with the University of South Carolina as a CM at Risk partner with Gilbane Construction Company on the University's New Law School.

Brownstone also continues to solidify its presence in the Columbia area by having the lead Program Management role in the renovation of Decker Center for Richland County. This much anticipated project will consolidate a number of the County's Courts and Sherriff's operations in the former Decker Mall and is expected to be a major component of the revitalization of this area.

Brownstone is also fortunate to be involved with the Richland County Transportation Penny program that will provide much needed transportation improvements throughout the County. This multi-year infrastructure improvement program will address roadways, streetscapes, bikeways, greenways and intersections throughout Richland County. As a lead partner on the 3-firm Program Development Team, Brownstone will lead management and design efforts in the areas of Procurement and Greenway Design.

Brownstone Design

Brownstone was recently proud to announce the addition of Architectural Services to our clients. Since its launch in 2012, Brownstone Design has initiated several projects in the Columbia area to include Upgrades at Crane Creek Park, Richland County Sports Complex Study and Additions and Renovations of CMRTA headquarters. With additional work in Allendale and Fairfield Counties, the design arm of Brownstone looks forward to the 2015 much anticipated completion of the Fairfield Career and Technology Center for nearby Fairfield County School District in Winnsboro, South Carolina.

Establishing Local Partnerships

Our Local, Small, Woman Owned and Minority Business Enterprise (LSWMBE) Outreach Efforts in the Columbia and other areas are second to none with documented results exceeding Owner goals on several projects. We have established ourselves as a "team player" with other MBE firms who see us as a partner in this effort instead of a direct competitor. Our track record has led to other MBE firms maintaining constant contact with our team as they are confident that they will have legitimate opportunities on our projects. In fact, several firms have written letters of support for Brownstone involvement on other projects as they understand that their opportunities will only increase if Brownstone is involved. This level of commitment has led to a "contractor following" that results in higher LSWMBE Participation rates for our clients.

Commitment to Excellence

While many are familiar with our very successful Management, Design and Outreach Efforts, we feel it imperative that our firm also be known for our "boots on the ground" efforts to complete projects. To this end, we have expanded our portfolio to provide on-site personnel on Construction Management at Risk teams assigned to the work construction projects. With personnel in decision-making roles on each project, Brownstone has gained valuable experience that will allow the company to expand into other areas of construction in the future. Construction experts provided on these projects have included Project Managers, Assistant Superintendents, Quality Control Supervisors, Assistant Project Managers as well as Administrative personnel. These persons have accepted their assigned tasks and performed admirably for our clients in response to

Brownstone's "no pass-through" philosophy of providing legitimate services,. As a result, all Brownstone partnered projects to date have been completed on-

▲ Richland 2 Center for Achievement

time, within budget, with great quality and free of controversy for our Owners. The aforementioned University of South Carolina Law School will further establish our personnel in this form of construction delivery.

Looking Toward a Promising Future

South Carolina has afforded Brownstone Construction Group to grow at a manageable pace during our short history. With major projects ongoing in Columbia, Charleston and other locales, the state is both large enough to support our operations, while being small enough for us to respond immediately to client concerns within the same day, if necessary. The majority of our employees call South Carolina "home" and are excited to be part of what we're expecting to be a bright future. We look forward to many years of growth in the Columbia area as we will commit ourselves to providing professional and competent services for our clients.

Photo by Paul Ringger

Campbell Consulting Group

Comprehensive Strategies for Solutions and Success

arrell Campbell infused the wealth of experience he had gained in governmental affairs into the business he launched in 2005. A native of Bennettsville and a graduate of the University of South Carolina, Campbell had been working as a legislative aide in the state House and as an intern in the Governor's office. He began his lobbying career in 1999 working for the firm of Ogburn & Associates. Six years later, he founded Campbell Consulting Group as a pioneering public affairs firm that would combine

sophisticated strategies with traditional communication methods. The company today is a team of highly experienced and knowledgeable public affairs professionals and marketing specialists that combine incomparable issue and process expertise with a complete range of public affairs services.

Campbell Consulting's substantive expertise related to impacting the public policy process is unique as compared to other public affairs organizations. Since its inception, the professionals of the Campbell Consulting Group have been offering a wide range of direct lobbying services covering local, state, and federal government, as well as regulatory agencies. The company has also built an impressive reputation for providing issue advocacy services that involve media relations, grassroots mobilization, advocacy, and much more.

STRATEGIES THAT BRING SOLUTIONS

The exceptional value the Campbell team brings to solving major challenges related to public policy not only depend upon their ability to help their clients develop workable policy proposals, but also rely on the design of efficient and comprehensive message development and issue advocacy strategies which play an important role in successfully converting the proposals into law.

In the arena of Governmental Affairs, the Campbell team, from senior level staff to extraordinary young professionals, specializes in high profile causes at the junction of politics, business, and the media. They offer the most impactful lobbying strategies to assist Fortune 500, 100, mid-size firms and trade associations pass or defeat legislation and regulations. Working with CEO's, COO's, VP's, and mid-level managers, they develop winning strategies for their clients' legislative agendas; navigating through the legislative and regulatory process; tracking and analyzing legislation; securing appropriations; educating and lobbying public officials and agency executives; and developing coalitions to drive their clients' agendas at the Federal, State and Local levels.

Campbell Consulting Group's Business Development experience provides companies with business solutions, thus enhancing market and profits. Campbell provides market research, bid tracking, competitive and geopolitical intelligence, opportunity identification, partnership strategy, and market entry planning with an eye to growing and protecting their clients' market share.

"We recognize that causes need a voice to bring about desired changes and we are proud to think that we are doing our share to ensure that voices are heard at every level of government in the United States," states Darrell Campbell. "We help influence key decision makers and the powers that be in effecting tax repeals, getting subsidies, helping troubled industries and generally powering public opinion to influence change."

Darrell has a passion for family, community, volunteering, and providing opportunities for young people.

◄ *Darrell Campbell works to provide a voice for clients at all levels of government.*

▼ *Pictured at the Community Relations Council Gala are (left to right): Darrell Campbell, Henri Baskins and Marvin Lare.*

Inn at USC Wyndham Garden

Classic Southern Charm. 21st Century Amenities

▲ The Inn retains the home's historic library but provides updated amenities.

The hotel lobby boasts the home's original mahogany ceiling, walls, and custom hardwood floors. ▶

The library, original to the Black House, is almost completely intact today. ▶▼

The Inn's new construction followed strict design guidelines as not to impose on the historic University Hill Neighborhood's grandeur or charm. ▼

The City of Columbia was still a struggling teenager when South Carolina College (now the University of South Carolina) was founded in 1801. By the time the university was officially chartered a century later, the city and the educational institution that, in many ways, identified it had undergone a radical transformation. A focal point in 2005 at the celebration of the University's second century of service to the state and its people was the recognition of an historic home that is now the centerpiece of what has become the welcoming point for guests checking into the classic boutique hotel known as the Inn at USC Wyndham Garden.

A Dream Becomes Reality

The Cain-Matthews-Thompkins-Black House, located at 1619 Pendleton Street, is situated on land purchased in 1908 by John J. Cain from Alexander G. Morris. Though not an architect by profession, Cain expressed to his daughter, Mrs. Mortimer Cosby, that the building represented his life's dream. He designed it to ensure his stylistic preferences were predominate in the structure, including the Gothic touches he incorporated into the living room.

A builder by trade and a native of Virginia, Mr. Cain had moved to Columbia primarily to improve the health of his eldest son, but he also wanted to work on renovating the dome of the state capitol building. Quickly acquiring a reputation as a quality builder, he completed construction of a number of local buildings,

including the Jefferson Hotel, the Arcade Mall, and the Palmetto Building.

Cain was completing construction of the Jefferson Hotel as work began on what is now known as the Cain-Matthews-Thompkins-Black House. J. Pope Matthews, the president of a local bank, next inhabited the house in an interesting swapping of homes with the Cain family who was living on nearby Senate Street.

Following the Matthews family living at the address from 1918 to 1931, the home would change hands several times. Arthur S. Tompkins called the residence home for two years from 1932 to 1934 followed by Charles P. Richardson from 1935 to 1936. Louie W. VanBibber next lived in the home until 1939 when Tompkins and his wife again took possession. The couple's daughter

and son-in-law, Mr. and Mrs. George Black, were the next and final family to live in the home.

The home would remain a private residence until 1974 when the University of South Carolina planned to acquire the property and construct a parking garage on the site. Following a series of negotiations and legal wrangling, the University scrapped its plans

for the garage and opted for a site across Pickens Street.

In 2003, the USC Development Foundation and IMIC Hotels drafted plans for construction of the Inn at USC Wyndham Garden. A joint effort by the Historic Columbia Foundation and other preservationists succeeded in designating

the historic home as part of the hotel and today serves as its lobby.

THE INN AT USC TODAY

The Inn at USC Wyndham Garden in the heart of downtown Columbia overlooks the historic campus of the University of South Carolina. Just steps from the historic Horseshoe, the (continued on next page)

▲ *A wide, airy front porch, true to southern style, welcomes today's guests.*
◄▼ *The original den of the Black House featured a grand scale portrait of Mrs. Mary Black and her mother, Mrs. Arthur Tompkins, painted by Howard Chandler Christy.*
▼ *The exterior of the private residence as it appeared in a 1965 photo changed very little when it was converted to a public property.*

City of rivers, vistas, and dreams

▲ Visitors to the Inn appreciate the original leaded-glass windows and detailed vintage woodwork in the hotel lobby and bar.

▶▲ The hotel's large outdoor terrace is available for private functions.

Standard King hotel room. ▶▼

Standard double Queen hotel room. ▶▼▼

The gracious Mary Tompkins Suite is one of the many suite options available to guests at the Inn at USC Wyndham Garden. ▼

charming boutique property is conveniently located to many of the area's premier attractions, including Williams-Brice Stadium, the Colonial Center, the South Carolina Governor's Mansion, the South Carolina State House, the State Museum, and the Columbia Museum of Art. Visitors are also drawn to an eclectic blend of dining options to suit any taste and budget. Nearby entertainment magnets include popular gathering spots such as Five Points and the Congaree Vista district, a unique neighborhood featuring dining, shopping, live entertainment, and the arts.

The Inn is widely known for its rare blend of historic grandeur in upscale accommodations and impeccable service. A boutique hotel of 117 luxury guest rooms, the Inn combines the ambience and charm of the antebellum South with the most modern amenities sought by today's travelers. Each of the Inn's stylishly outfitted guestrooms and suites feature complimentary wireless high speed Internet access, plush pillow-top king or queen-size beds, coffee makers, refrigerators, microwaves, and premium cable television.

The visitor is quickly embraced by the Inn's true Southern hospitality that creates a warm, comfortable feeling normally found in a quaint bed and breakfast. Close attention to detail has created the feel of visiting a stately Southern mansion. A complimentary, cooked-to-order hot breakfast of traditional favorites along with a well-equipped fitness center is available. Guests also enjoy relaxing in a rocking chair on the Inn's front porch and meeting friends at the afternoon social.

A PRESTIGIOUS BUSINESS ADDRESS

In addition to its myriad attractions for leisure travelers, the

Inn at USC Wyndham Garden has also become widely known as the classic location of choice for meeting planners searching for the perfect location to conduct business in the Palmetto State. The Inn's more than 3,000 square feet of flexible meeting and banquet space can be configured in a wide variety of seating arrangements.

The Inn's staff works closely with event coordinators to ensure the success of meetings, seminars, conferences, cocktail receptions, birthday parties, rehearsal dinners, anniversary parties, wedding receptions and other special events.

A historic landmark. A prestigious venue for business meetings. A boutique hotel focused on customer service. The Inn at USC Wyndham Garden looks forward to a bright future of serving the people of Columbia and the local business community as well as the thousands who visit each year to absorb the city's rich cultural heritage and enjoy its numerous attractions.

◄▲ Meeting planners are invited to take advantage of the conference rooms and meeting spaces, including The Carolina Room with its seating for up to 100 attendees.

Presidential Suites include original windows and fireplaces. Though non-functioning now, the fireplaces and mantels help retain the character of the home. Wet bars have also been added. ◄▼

Many suites feature separate living rooms, marble tile and garden tubs. ◄▼▼

▲ Guests can keep up wellness goals using onsite fitness facilities as well as with their access to the best full-service gym in Columbia.

The Inn at USC Wyndham Garden offers a choice of 34 suites; some featuring balconies, vaulted ceilings, wet bars, whirlpool tubs or fireplaces. With such a variety of options, the Inn can customize any visit. ▼

Meet our Photographers

Bill Barley

After earning a degree in photo-illustration from Rochester Institute of Technology, Bill Barley began his career as a photojournalist. In 1966, he opened a studio from which he has since provided photography for corporations, ad agencies, and design firms throughout South Carolina.

Today, with four decades of experience, he specializes in aerial, advertising, and business photography. He also produces high quality Giclée prints of his work as well as for numerous regional artists.

He maintains professional affiliations with the American Society of Media Photographers, Professional Photographers of America, Professional Photographers of SC, Aircraft Owners and Pilots Association and the Lexington Chamber of Commerce.

bill@billbarley.com

billbarley.com

803 755-1554 office

803 755-3711 fax

803 960-8198 cell

Jay Browne

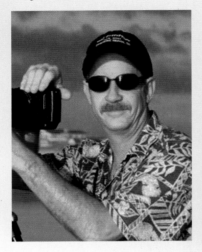

Jay Browne, a native South Carolinian, bought his first camera in Hawaii to record surfing and scenics in the early '70's.

From there his passion for and expertise at his craft led him to turn professional in 1989. Since then, he has operated a studio in Columbia.

An avid outdoorsman, a drummer and guitarist, golfer, and collector of Japanese maples, his body of work is extensive and diverse; characteristics demonstrated by his treatments of architecture, fine art, portraits, aerials, stock photos, interiors, editorial, photo workshops, weddings, nature, products, real estate, and skylines.

His contagious playfulness coaxes his subjects to look their best, and all his work is done with a patience and panache that are his hallmarks.

jayandturbo@gmail.com

803-351-9986

Ron Cogswell

Ron Cogswell is COO of The Civil War Trust (www.civilwar.org), the nation's largest private-sector organization preserving American Civil War battlefields, including Chattanooga and Chickamauga. Ron lives in Arlington, Va., with his wife, Beth.

Originally from Chicago, he served in the U.S. Navy from 1969-1972, and became an amateur digital photographer in 2001 after being taught the basics and more by the great and patient Elliot Cohen.

civilwar.org

rcogswell@msn.com

Helen Evans

A native of Colby, Wisconsin, Helen Evans lives in Irmo, SC, with her husband and twin boys. Having bought her first camera in only 2012, Helen's talent has been recognized from the outset with exhibits in a number of juried art shows and online photography forums.

Busy with her growing business, Amazin' Gracie Photography, she loves urban exploration and photographing abandoned/historic buildings and properties. A member of several photo groups, including the Columbia Camera Club, she plans to pursue her PPA certification.

"I'm blessed with the opportunities God has thrown my way, and so very thankful to be doing something I love".

agphoto@yahoo.com

facebook.com/amazingraciephotography

http://amazingraciephotography.zenfolio.com/

803-603-7635

Bruce Flashnick

Originally from New York City, Bruce Flashnick perspicaciously decided to move to South Carolina in 1974.

At the age of 14, he had already developed a passion for photography and has followed that passion ever since.

With over 40 years of professional photography experience, he enjoys showcasing the beauty that is South Carolina—his chosen home.

bruceflashnick@me.com

bruceflashnick.com

803-238-0605 cell

Sam Holland

Beginning a career as a newspaper photographer, his award winning style gained Sam Holland the opportunity to be the stills photographer on a motion picture. This break led to an additional vocation as a film location scout and manager.

Currently, Sam serves as photographer for the South Carolina House of Representatives, which has allowed him to meet and photograph some remarkable people, as he recalls, "One day, lined up to be regconized in the House Chamber, we had a space shuttle pilot, all of the Miss South Carolina Pageant contestents and 'The Godfather of Soul,' James Brown."

scimages.com

movisearch@me.com

803-920-2291

John Nelson

A native of Columbia, John Nelson is a botanist and the Curator of the A. C. Moore Herbarium at the University of South Carolina (www.herbarium.org). He admits that his knowledge of the theory behind photography is… well, minimal. Nevertheless, he is a prodigious picture-taker, and many of his most interesting photos may be seen on flickr.com, under the name "Just Back".

flickr.com/photos/32998163@N00/

johnbnelson@sc.rr.com

Stephanie Norwood

A Memphis-area native, Stephanie Norwood studied Graphic Design and Fine Art at Parsons The New School for Design in New York City.

She takes a photojournalistic approach to her lifestyle and fine art photography and specializes in portraits, figure, cultural events, and architecture. Stephanie developed her passion for photography during a 30-year career as an international model.

Her work has been featured in *Cork It*, Memphis' *Downtowner* magazine, *Memphis* magazine, and *Knoxville: Green by Nature*.

Studio Norwood Photography
www.StudioNorwood.com

info@StudioNorwood.com

901-217-2509

Moore Photographers on page 236

City of rivers, vistas, and dreams

Tom Poland

Paul Ringger

Tom Poland first considered photography as a career but soon realized his talent lay in writing. More than that, legal pads and pens proved much more affordable than cameras, lens, and accessories. Many years later, digital cameras came to his rescue. He's often in the field researching unusual wildlife habitat, histories, and classic back-road venues, and he never leaves his camera behind. (Note the camera around his neck.) Now and then he admits he gets lucky. Photographed here by Robert C. Clark, he sits amid a colony of pitcher plants in a remote and wild South Carolina wetland known as a Red Bluff bay.

tompoland.net

tompol@earnlink.net

Publisher's Note:

Yes, this intrepid photographer is the self-same individual who is the author of this book.

The abstract realism of Paul Ringger's photo-art has a large following on Facebook. This is no surprise to those whose work he has supported as a software engineer specializing in digital communication. Countless users of graphic and text systems have long been dependent on solutions such as those he delivered as leader of the world's first production team integrating text and graphics for print in the early 90s. His skills are equally leading edge today and are employed by some of the foremost technical companies on the planet.

His long-time study of the visual arts and the physics of their digital conveyance, has recently led to the creation of his impressive art portfolio.

facebook.com/paulringger

paul.ringger@gmail.com

Photo by Paul Ringger